'And Who Will Make the Chapatis ?'

A village woman once asked her husband if she could attend a training camp on panchayats.
'And who will make the chapatis ?' he asked.

Members of Bitargaon's all-women panchayat

'AND WHO WILL MAKE THE CHAPATIS ?'

A Study of All-Women Panchayats in Maharashtra

Edited by
BISHAKHA DATTA

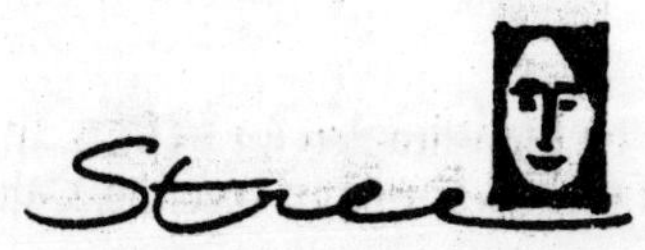

'AND WHO WILL MAKE THE CHAPATIS?' : A Study of
All-Women Panchayats in Maharashtra, edited by Bishakha Datta
was first published in May 1998 by Stree
16 Southern Avenue, Calcutta 700 026

Reprinted 2000

ISBN 81-85604-24-X

Distributed by
Popular Prakashan Pvt. Ltd.
Mumbai, Calcutta, Delhi, Pune

Typesetting and design by
LOGS, 6 Ram Hari Mistry Lane, Calcutta 700 013
and printed by Arora Offset Press

Published by Mandira Sen for STREE, an imprint of
Bhatkal and Sen, 16 Southern Avenue, Calcutta 700 026

CONTENTS

ACKNOWLEDGEMENTS

This study of all-women panchayats grew out of the increasing recognition of the need for women to participate in politics. None of this would have happened without the hospitality of the women's panchayats, whose members shared their political experiences with us over many memorable meals. It is to them that we owe our deepest thanks. The book was written mainly by Bishakha Datta with significant contributions from Meenakshi Shedde, Sharmila Joshi and Sonali Sathaye. The photographs were provided by Gautam Ojha, Mangesh Nardekar, Neela Kapadia and Purnima Rao. The study would not have been possible without the generous support of the Ford Foundation. We would sincerely like to thank Jane Rosser of the Ford Foundation in this respect.

Thanks are also due to a range of people who facilitated the study in other ways. Lalita Kolharkar, Swapnali Das, Sheetal Karmakar, Kshama Deshpande and Sushma Shaligram undertook the time-consuming task of translating and transcribing mountains of taped Marathi interviews into English. Ramya Subrahmanian constantly shared with us her vast and updated collection of resource materials on gender, which has contributed to developing our conceptual framework.

We were helped along by the support, encouragement and feedback of Medha Kotwal Lele and Simrita Gopal Singh of Aalochana. Hazel D'Lima's 1980-study on women in Panchayati Raj yielded the wonderful quote that we have used as the title for our study.

Finally, a very special thanks to Gautam Ojha, for pushing this work to its finish. We never really believed it would happen.

MAP. ALL-WOMEN PANCHAYATS IN MAHARASHTRA

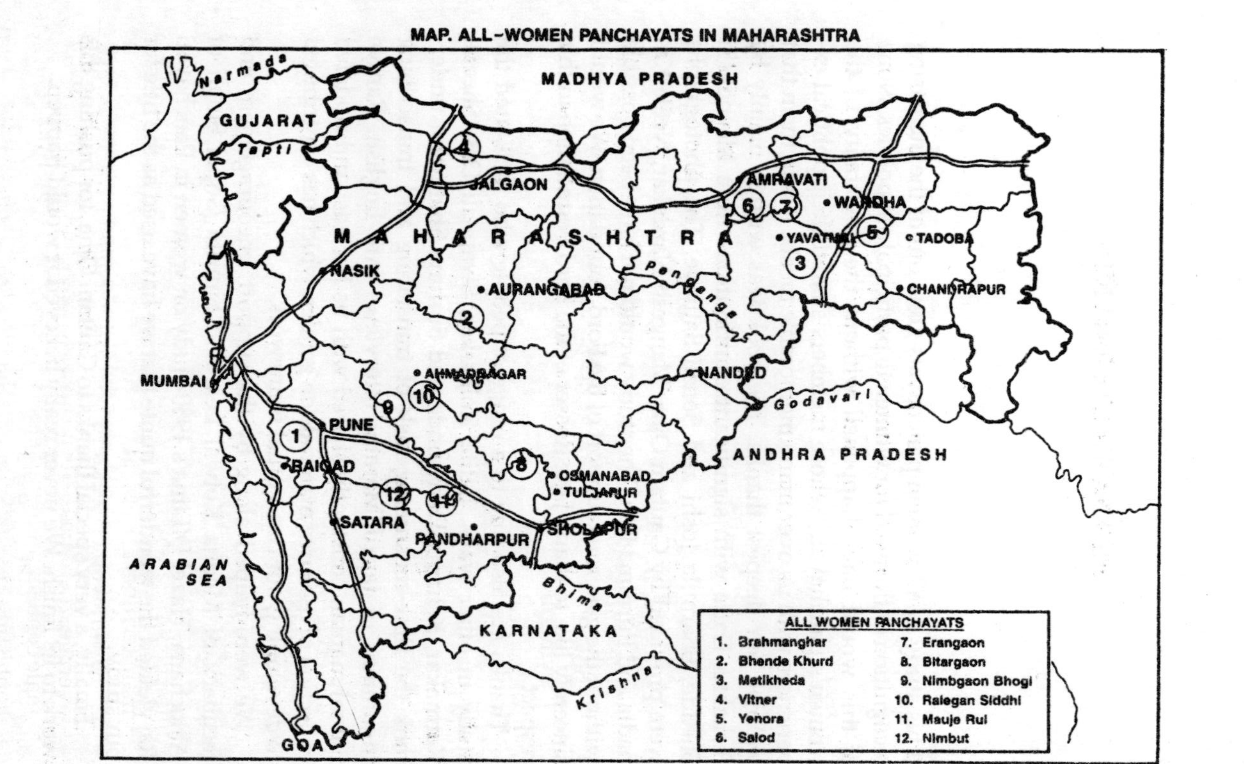

INTRODUCTION

'And who will make the chapatis?'

BACKGROUND

Women and politics

Women are virtually excluded from political power all over the world. Although women constitute half the population, only 3.5 percent of the world's cabinet ministers are women, and women hold no ministerial positions in 93 countries. All political systems, regardless of ideology or form, routinely deny women formal political status. As writer and researcher Maxine Molyneux observes:

> Politics, more than any other realm, because of its condensation of power and authority, has remained largely a monopoly of men. This is so empirically, as evidenced by the miniscule percentage of women occupying political power in every country of the world. But it is also true symbolically in that the attributes considered necessary for political effectiveness are seen as quintessentially masculine. As a consequence, political women. . . are seen as the deviants, the trespassers or the guests in a terrain which does not fundamentally belong to them.[1]

In India too, electoral politics continues to remain a male preserve, both empirically and symbolically. Male voters have consistently outnumbered women voters by 11 percent over the last five Indian elections although this gap is narrowing; one psephologist considers that only 30 percent of female voters are 'aware voters.'[2] That such a term is rarely used to describe uninformed male voters only indicates that politics is still considered male territory.

Fewer women contest political positions than men. On an average, there have been three women candidates for every 100 male contestants in past elections. Only 200 of the 9,107 candidates contesting the 1989 Lok Sabha elections were women. Though major political parties now promise to reserve 30 percent of their seats for women, their record shows otherwise: in the 1989 elections, women comprised 9.9 percent of Congress candidates, 6.6 percent of BJP candidates, 5.5 percent of CPI/CPI(M) candidates, and 3.4 percent of Janata Dal candidates.

Lower participation ensures that women remain under-represented in politics at all levels. Before Independence, women constituted 10 percent of those jailed for protesting British rule, the pivotal form of political activity at that time. Since then, women have never held more than 8 percent of the seats in the Lok Sabha, even though in absolute terms the number of women Members of Parliament has risen from 22 in 1951 to 36 in 1991. 'It was easier to get arrested for supporting democracy than it is to get elected to the democratic institutions that Indian nationalists were fighting to obtain,' note political science professors Barbara Nelson and Najma Chowdhury.[3]

If women are marginalized in politics at national and state levels, they are practically absent in villages, which are more tradition-bound. All-women panchayats at the village levels—the subject of this study—are clearly an anomaly in a country where women have so little political power. The importance of creating women's panchayats at the village level received formal recognition in the mid-seventies, when the Committee on the Status of Women in India recommended the establishment of statutory women's panchayats at the village level. This was seen as a transitional measure to ensure greater participation by rural women in the political process.

This recommendation coincided with growing worldwide recognition of the need for women to participate in politics. Although the United Nations had adopted a Convention on the Political Rights of Women as early as 1952, this issue had received little real attention. In 1985, the Declaration at the World Conference of Women in Nairobi, noted that 'for true equality to become a reality for women, the sharing of power on equal terms with men must be a major strategy.' This gave some impetus to the critical issue of women's political participation.

In India too, the women's movement has given little priority to the issue of women's participation in electoral politics until relatively recently. The movement has yet to evolve a coherent position or a coordinated strategy on this issue, but there have been a few isolated regional initiatives in this arena. Some groups, including the National Commission on Women, had earlier called for reservation of seats for women; a few women's groups like the Bangalore-based Vimochana campaigned against politicians in the 1989 general elections, and many women's groups in Ahmedabad, Bangalore and Pune prepared women's manifestos in the eighties.

'Women and politics' has emerged as an important issue only in this decade. This theme was discussed at the 1990 National Women's Conference held at Kozhikode. The possibility of forming a women's party was also touched on. A few networks have since formed around the issue of women's political participation. But autonomous women's groups still remain uncertain whether a continuing struggle within formal political structures is more effective than the struggle for women's rights from outside the system.

In this vacuum, government enactments have provided the greatest fillip to the issue of women's participation in electoral politics. Both Karnataka and Maharashtra reserved seats for women at the local and state levels in the eighties. The 1992 enactment of the Seventy-Third Amendment—which reserves 33 percent of seats for women on Panchayati Raj institutions—has suddenly brought this issue into national focus. More than 800,000 women are expected to enter politics as a result. Realizing the need to equip these women with political skills, a spectrum of women's groups and non-governmental organizations (NGOs) are currently engaged in researching, documenting and training women to enter electoral politics. This study hopes to contribute and feed into this ongoing process.

Women and Panchayati Raj

Although panchayats had existed in India long before British rule, Panchayati Raj—the formal system of local self-government—came into being only after Independence. Panchayati Raj found no place in the Constitution that was then being drafted. Instead, it was tucked away in the Directive Principles of State Policy (Article 40). Several states set up Panchayati Raj bodies at village, block and district levels in the late fifties. These were seen primarily as participatory mechanisms to achieve rapid rural development in the conditions of a democracy in the making. But these bodies soon started languishing in the absence of constitutional support, political will and adequate powers and resources.

Women were rarely found on these bodies, except as co-opted members who got little power, respect or political status.

During this time, many commissions were set up to strengthen Panchayati Raj mechanisms. Most notable among these are the Balwant Rai Mehta Study Team (1957), the Ashok Mehta Committee (1977), the G.V.K. Rao Committee (1985), and the L.M. Singhvi Committee (1987). Panchayati Raj was also mentioned in the Seventh Five Year Plan. In 1988, a parliamentary subcommittee recommended that Panchayati Raj bodies be given constitutional recognition. Two constitutional amendments to do so—the Sixty-Fourth and the Seventy-Fourth—never took off, but in 1992, Parliament approved the Seventy-Third Amendment.

This amendment, which finally gives Panchayati Raj constitutional status, has been hailed for its provisions. These require each state to establish gram sabhas, hold periodic elections, set up three tiers of Panchayati Raj (if the state population exceeds 20 lakhs) and establish a statutory State Finance Commission for these bodies. Side by side, the Eleventh Schedule lists 29 subjects for which Panchayati Raj institutions will now be responsible. The provision which has most significance for women is the reservation of 33 percent seats for women on Panchayati Raj bodies at all levels. Maharashtra and Karnataka had earlier passed such acts, which prompted a mass of women to enter these bodies. Despite this enabling provision, critics point out that these bodies have still not been given enough functions, powers or resources to shape them as effective units of self-government.

Panchayati Raj in Maharashtra

Maharashtra, the state in which our study is based, follows a three-tier system of Panchayati Raj. This consists of:

(i) gram panchayats at the village level
(minimum population: 600)
(ii) panchayat samitis at the block level
(one block = many villages)
(iii) zilla parishads at the district level
(one district = many blocks)

Gram panchayats constitute the most basic unit of decentralized decision-making in India today. Each gram panchayat has between seven to fifteen members, depending on the village population; villages with less than 600 population are clubbed with neighbouring villages to form group panchayats. The sarpanch, who leads the panchayat, is separately elected by panchayat members. Gram panchayats, which have a term of five years, are elected by and accountable to the gram sabha—the adult electorate of each village. The gram sabha is mandatorily required to meet twice a year to endorse panchayat decisions, but this happens more in theory than in practice. A gram sevak, who is a government employee, administers the work of each panchayat, and jointly signs cheques with the sarpanch.

Although gram panchayats are legally empowered to collect taxes and keep them—Maharashtra's panchayats collect house, water and electricity taxes—these constitute a miniscule proportion of panchayat budgets. Taxes are used not to initiate development schemes, but for minor maintenance-related expenditures. Development schemes are funded through grants from the central and state governments, which constitute the major sources of panchayat funds. Perhaps the single biggest source of gram panchayat funding today is the Jawahar Rozgar Yojana (JRY), which was introduced to combat rural unemployment in 1989. All gram panchayats receive funds annually under JRY; amounts vary according to village population.

Other central and state government schemes such as Indira Awas Yojana (IAY), and Jeevan Dhara are prominent sources of panchayat funding. Gram panchayats also administer poverty-alleviating programmes like the Integrated Rural Development Programme (IRDP). Typically, gram panchayats must write proposals to the panchayat samiti or zilla parishad to get funds under different schemes.

Maharashtra has more than 25,000 gram panchayats today. Elections to Maharashtra's gram panchayats have been held seven times since 1962; the last one was held in 1995. Reservation of 33 percent seats has empowered at least two women from each village to participate in the recent gram panchayat elections.

All-Women Panchayats

A few all-women panchayats are known to have existed after Independence in Karnataka, Orissa, Madhya Pradesh and Maharashtra. Our study focuses on documenting the experiences of

Maharashtra's all-women panchayats. The first-known women's panchayat in Maharashtra was formed in 1962 at Nimbut, a village in the sugar belt of Pune district. Chronic water scarcity prompted another such panchayat to be formed in 1984 in Mauje Rui village in the same district. During this time, women such as freedom-fighter Usha Nikam set up all-women panels during elections in villages like Indoli and Palshi, both in Satara district. These experiences were documented in journals like *Manushi*.

It was only during the 1989 elections that eight women's panchayats simultaneously came to power, largely at the initiative of activists of the Shetkari Sanghatana. The Sanghatana, a Maharashtra-based peasant movement, had earlier given a call for rural women to enter politics. Sanghatana activists spontaneously formed women's panels in five villages in response to this. These villages are: Salod and Erangaon in Amravati district, Yenora in Wardha district, Metikheda in Yavatmal district, and Vitner in Jalgaon district.

The three other women's panchayats that came to power in 1989—in Nimbgaon Bhogi in Pune district, Ralegan Siddhi in Ahmednagar district, and Bitargaon in Solapur district—did so at the initiative of local political leaders, including women. Ralegan is notable as the village where social reformer Anna Hazare based his development efforts, while Nimbgaon is known more for the political connections of its sarpanch, Usha Badhe. In Bitargaon, all the nine women who came to power are illiterate. In 1992, two more women's panchayats came to power and are still functioning. One of these—at Bhende Khurd in Ahmednagar—was used by a sugar baron to maintain his hold on local political institutions. The other panchayat, elected in Brahmanghar in Pune district, is really run by women.

Our study documents and critically analyses the experiences of the twelve all-women panchayats that came to power in Maharashtra (see Map preceding Introduction). A table of these panchayats follows the Introduction (see Table).

THE STUDY

This nine-month qualitative study of all-women panchayats was indirectly triggered off by a newspaper article headlined 'We Want to Outdo the Males'. Flanked by a group photograph of 11 unsmiling women self-consciously posing for the camera, the article went on to describe how a women's panchayat had revolutionized Pidghara village in Madhya Pradesh in 1989. How had rural women come to power in one of India's most backward states? A rummage through libraries for traces of similar panchayats in Maharashtra—considered one of India's more affluent, progressive states—yielded two findings. One, that 12 women's panchayats had been or were in existence among the state's 25,000 panchayats. Two, that there was very little documented evidence of their existence. In short, they could have come and gone and no one would ever have known.

This study hopes to rectify that omission to some extent. Hazel D'Lima's 1980 study examined the role of women at the higher levels of Panchayati Raj—zilla parishads and panchayat samitis.[4] Our study adds to this by looking at women on the lowest rung of Panchayati Raj. This is perhaps the first field-based research study of all-women panchayats in Maharashtra. We hope it will serve to voice, visibilize and validate the experiences of women on them—and contribute to the small but vital body of action research on women in rural politics. The study is presented in two sections. The first part looks at all panchayats barring the Shetkari Sanghatana panchayats, which are clubbed together in the second section. Different panchayats are documented at varying levels of detail.

FRAMEWORK

The study critically examines these panchayats from a women's perspective, intertwining elements of rural sociology, politics, and feminism. Our starting point is the broader definition of politics put forward by the women's movement:

> The collective action of women against oppressive patriarchal power with the long-term goal of social transformation that would ensure women's rights and their liberation from subjugation, superstition, degradation and injustice.[5]

Given this perspective, the study primarily concerns itself with one broad question: Have all-women panchayats carved out a political space that allows women to transform their lives?

Several issues are examined as part of this inquiry:

What is the status of women in this area? What is the history of women's participation in political and social movements?
How was each panchayat formed? What was the role of men, political parties, violence, money, caste, class in the formation of each panchayat?
What are the dynamics among women on the panchayats? How far is each woman's role and functioning determined by caste, class, education, culture, previous experience of activism, gender dynamics and so on?
How does an all-women panchayat function vis-à-vis a mixed panchayat? How does power, leadership, decision-making manifest itself in either case?
What issues do all-women panchayats choose to address? Do these issues address the concerns of the women in the village? Do such panchayats address women's issues such as rape, domestic violence which mixed panchayats consider outside their purview?
What impact have such panchayats had on the village women in terms of empowerment?
What impact has being on the panchayat had on a woman's life at home? How does her private role (as wife and mother) interact with her public role (as elected official)? Has one influenced the other?
How far have women on these panchayats created a political space which can be used to transform women's lives? How can this space be widened, their participation made more meaningful?

METHODOLOGY

Our nine-month qualitative study began in the summer of 1994 when many of the panchayats still had one year left of their term. Two of us, Sharmila and Bishakha, both journalists, started off the project through a quick survey of all the villages. On the basis of this, we decided to study in detail three villages with a greater potential for women's empowerment. These villages are Bitargaon, Vitner and Metikheda. It was agreed that we would also document the experiences of other villages in less detail.

Fieldwork began only after the humid summer heat had been washed away by the monsoon. Each of us took responsibility for researching one village in detail. This meant spending at least two weeks in the village and attending panchayat meetings and gram sabhas where possible. Sonali, an anthropology student who joined the project at this stage, also took on a similar responsibility. Sharmila went to Bitargaon, Bishakha to Metikheda and Sonali to Vitner. Side by side, we continued to visit other villages, meet panchayat officials and women's groups. One of the panchayats—Nimbgaon Bhogi—was discovered purely through a chance meeting with a Zilla Parishad official.

Although all three of us identify with and share the goals of the women's movement, we would hesitate placing ourselves within the movement except in a very broad sense. Each of us has links with the movement and has participated in its struggles, but we see ourselves primarily as individuals with a variety of goals, concerns and influences. The women's movement is merely one, albeit an important one, of these influences.

In the field, qualitative interviews were done very informally—a questionnaire was carted along as a checklist but rarely used. Interviews were done at the women's convenience, over lunch, dinner, in the field, or while putting a baby to sleep. Whenever the women got fed up with talking about panchayats, we would talk of this and that. They seem to have enjoyed the interviews—going by the number of repeat dinner invitations we received.

A visual component was soon added to our study in a spontaneous manner, mainly because we feel that visuals are accessible, communicate easily, and add life and energy to a documentation project. Frankly, it is enjoyable to see the faces of people you read about. Professional photographers were enlisted for this exercise, which soon took on its own momentum. In Bitargaon, sarpanch Nani Lawand dressed and posed as a man for the camera. In Brahmanghar, fifty women enthusiastically recreated a road construction sequence.

The women took to the photographs like nothing on earth. Every time we went back to a village, which we mostly did, we took copies along with us. That these 5x3 postcard prints forged bonds like nothing else only goes to show that technology does have its uses. The second visit, which made the villagers feel like we hadn't just come, taken and gone, often yielded the real gems in terms of research data.

Very rarely did we face any problems, either with women or with their husbands. When husbands spoke on behalf of their wives, we let them speak—and then said we wanted to chat with their wives. This non-confrontational request was always acceded to and we were left in peace with the women. In some villages, where we found we had to stay with the rural elite, honesty turned out to be the best policy to explain this decision to marginal groups. We often could not gauge income levels—a sarpanch who owns 30 acres of land but has only three raggedy sarees: is she rich or poor? We presented her with a saree after we had sponged several meals off her. Village women are very fastidious about the kind of saree they wear—each *pallu*, border, shade and style has a caste and regional connotation—so we ended up changing the saree three times, but that's another story.

As the fieldwork came to a close with the gram panchayat elections of 1995, which we attended in Metikheda, we were left with a slew of formal recordings and an informal mosaic of images from the past. The amount of train tickets we booked and changed, delayed and cancelled trains, even the train we missed at Bitargaon still stays with us. Meenakshi, who came into the project at its last stage, remembers changing twelve vehicles to get to Mauje Rui. Bishakha recalls singing '*Sasa re Sasa*' (Rabbit, O Rabbit) with Brahmanghar's children at the village temple.

The most enduring images are those of the women. If in Vitner, it is Gujjar women dancing in abandon at a wedding party, in Brahmanghar it is groups of women playing *phugdi* during a photo-session. If in Bhende, it's the sarpanch's drunk husband, in Metikheda it's the women gathering to protect their sarpanch at a time of crisis. One of the most enduring images is that of Brahmanghar's Mandakini Dhumal, nonchalantly ignoring her brother-in-law's repeated commands to go fetch the cattle, now!

Tangled with the memories are occasional skeins of discomfort that it is comforting to label dissonance. Who are we—urban, privileged, affluent—to criticize Nimbgaon's sarpanch—rural, privileged, affluent—when in an absolute sense, we are representatives of the same class as her?

There are many more things to say, but a word about language is all that's needed before we end. We have tried to avoid the language of development as much as possible, mainly because we believe its dull, generalized tone does not reflect the grit, reality and sparkle of these women's lives. As far as possible, we have tried to retain the women's voices, liberally peppering the narrative with quotes.

Mumbai, 1998 B.D.

Table : ALL-WOMEN PANCHAYATS IN MAHARASHTRA

Name of Village	District	Point of Interest	Term	Sarpanch
BRAHMANGHAR taluka Bhor	Pune	Most men have migrated out	1992-97	Pushpalata Dhumal
BHENDE KHURD taluka Newasa	Ahmednagar	A farce; male-dominated	1992-97	Kusum Nawle
METIKHEDA taluka Ralegaon	Yavatmal	Shetkari Sanghatana elected	1989-94	Maiah Wankhede
VITNER taluka Chopda	Jalgaon	Shetkari Sanghatana, land transferred to women	1989-94	Shubha Raisingh
YENORA taluka Hinganghat	Wardha	Shetkari Sanghatana	1989-94	Ujwala Rishi Gote
SALOD taluka Nandgaon-Khandeshwar	Amravati	Shetkari Sanghatana	1989-94	Sairabi Sattar Khan
ERANGAON taluka Nandgaon-Khandeshwar	Amravati	Shetkari Sanghatana, two men on panchayat	1989-94	Anjana Toras
BITARGAON taluka Mhada	Solapur	Fully illiterate panchayat	1989-94	Satyabhama Lawand
NIMBGAON BHOGI taluka Shirur	Pune	Four women resigned	1989-94	Usha Badhe
RALEGAON SIDDHI taluka Parner	Ahmednagar	Village went through major social reform	1989-94	Contact Anna Hazare
MAUJE RUI taluka Indapur	Pune	Older panchayat	1984-89	Padmavati Ramchandra Kare
NIMBUT taluka Baramati	Pune	Oldest known all-women panchayat	1963-68	Kamal Babulal Kakade

NOTES

1. Maxine Molyneux, Introduction to 'Women in Popular Movements : India and Thailand During the Decade of Women', edited by Gail Omvedt, United Nations Research Unit for Social Development (1986)
2. Sakina Yusuf Khan, 'Sorry, It's a Stag Party', *Times of India* (19 May 1991)
3. Barbara Nelson and Najma Chowdhury, *Women and Politics Worldwide*, Boston: Yale University Press, (1994)
4. Hazel D'Lima, *Women In Local Government: A Study of Maharashtra*, Mumbai: Nirmala Niketan College of Social Work, (1984)
5. Vibhuti Patel, ed., 'Getting a Foothold in Politics' in *Readings on Women Studies* Series No.5, Mumbai: Research Centre for Women's Studies, SNDT University

Part I

Sarpanch Satyabhama 'Nani' Lawand dressed up as a man

NIMBUT

Meenakshi Shedde

'If I can run the house, why not a panchayat?'

Nimbut is a nondescript village in Pune district's Baramati taluka, a sugar belt taluka where local sugar barons like Sharad Pawar control local politics. Nimbut is the sort of village that introduces itself—when the clouds of dust raised by the State Transport bus have settled down—through a goat tied to a flat stone under a thorny tree. The tiny swaths of black hair around it announce that the stone is, in fact, the village barber's chair. From the stone, a path strays to the village, which has about 4,500 residents, mostly Maratha farmers.

'Although our village has earned many victories in *kusti* (wrestling) competitions and bullock cart races, it is proudest of the fact that it elected an all-women panchayat way back in 1963,' says a villager, Rajkumar Kerba Bansode. The election was indeed a landmark, creating history almost three decades before the government formally enacted legislation to ensure that women are represented in Panchayati Raj institutions.

When Nimbut elected thirteen women to its panchayat in 1963—the first known all-women panchayat in Maharashtra—Panchayati Raj was itself a relatively new concept. Most states had passed legislation to establish panchayats only in 1959, two years after the Balwantrai Mehta Committee Report of 1957 had emphasised the need for 'democratic decentralization'. In villages like Nimbut—which had elected only two panchayats thus far—men were still grappling with the full implications of what it meant for hitherto inconsequential people like themselves to be voted to power for five years. An all-women panchayat seemed a distant phenomenon.

Kamalbai Babulal Kakade, who was sarpanch of that all-women panchayat, is also the key to that unlikely phenomenon. (But like every other woman in Nimbut, Kamalbai cannot be located without mention of her husband's name, Babulal, as her middle name.) In her youth, Kamalbai was an unusually spirited woman, who learnt to swim, ride horses and drive a car, though educated only till Class IV in a school where the same teacher taught Classes I to IV. The election of an all-women panchayat was really a spontaneous expression of her will—achieved through the unstinting support of the powerful family she married into—not a premeditated strategy to empower women.

At the age of 17, Kamalbai was married into the Kakade household, a highly respected family of landlords, who owned 800 to 900 acres of sugarcane fields and controlled the nearby 2,200-member strong Someshwar Sugar Cooperative. The clan also controlled political power: a Kakade has been the sarpanch of every gram panchayat till today. As patrons of the village, the Kakades influenced all major village decisions. Villagers would bring their woes and quarrels to be sorted out at their house, Kamalbai recalls, and she would listen in on these sessions. One day she announced quietly that she would like to be on the next gram panchayat. 'If I can run the house, why not a panchayat?' she reasoned.

One might not think that managing a house particularly qualifies one to manage a panchayat, but running the Kakade household was a feat in itself. The Kakades were an enormous joint family: Kamalbai inherited three mothers-in-law, four brothers-in-law and each of their families—all under one roof. When her husband Babulal's parents died at a relatively young age, she took on the responsibility of looking after the entire household. So seriously did she take this duty that from 1954 to 1961, Kamalbai went to live in Pune with her husband's younger brothers so that they, along with her own children, could be better educated there.

Kamalbai's overriding dedication to her family responsibilities earned her not just respect and affection, but the support needed to form her own panchayat. Most crucially, she obtained her husband, Babulal's support and that of his liberal step-brother, Mukutrao Sahebrao, then chairman of the powerful Someshwar Sugar Cooperative. When Kamalbai said she would be more at ease with other women, rather than men, on the panchayat, the Kakades instructed villagers to put up their wives as election candidates—and to vote for them. Most of these women were illiterate and diffident, but Kamalbai rallied them around with a 'Come on, I'm just like you—I've studied only till Class IV too.'

There was much apprehension about the election results. 'We sat up till they finished counting the votes at one in the morning, and some of the women were really frightened,' Kamalbai recounts. All the thirteen women candidates were elected, and all the men defeated. 'When we won, I told my brothers-in-law to write my victory speech, but I couldn't even read it out properly. I was so excited,' says Kamalbai. 'But I'd read that when Gandhiji was felicitated on becoming a barrister, and asked to make a speech, he could only mumble "Bandhuon-bhagininon, bandhuon-bhagininon. . . [Brothers and sisters. . .]" It was a great honour for me to become sarpanch of an all-women panchayat at a time when Indira Gandhi had not even become the prime minister of India.'

Now in her seventies, Kamalbai speaks in unhurried, considered tones, her mien marked with an unmistakable, aristocratic grace. In its five-year term, she says, the women's panchayat

i. built a panchayat office with Rs 5,000 specially sanctioned for the purpose by her supportive brother-in-law, who was also head of the district credit cooperative society;
ii. built a wall for the school well;
iii. bought 10 acres of land to supplement panchayat funds; and
iv. brought electricity to the village in 1965, when it was sanctioned to reach them only in 1975.

The panchayat also ushered in a period of relative calm. There were fewer quarrels in the village because the men were too embarrassed to have their quarrels sorted out by a woman sarpanch! The five years in office were intoxicating for Kamalbai. 'I felt good going all the way to Baramati to meet the Block Development Officer,' she says. 'When we had to get clearances for various village projects, we got our work done faster because the bureaucrats would feel bad to ask a lady to call on them again—and a *khandani stree* (aristocratic woman) at that.' When she couldn't handle things on her own, Kamalbai would take the gram sevak's help or persuade her husband to go to Pune to liaise with the government on her behalf.

How do others remember this wondrous aberration thirty-two years on? Four of the 13 panchayat members have passed away. Many of the others have migrated to other villages. Vatsalabai Dhondiba Pharande, a former panchayat member now in her mid-sixties, lives in Pharandenagar nearby. *'Aata kashala?'* (Why rake it up now?), she retorts querulously, when asked to recall her term as a member of the historic, earliest recorded all-woman panchayat of 1963. She had no idea it was a first, and she couldn't care less. 'Oh, we built roads, lit them up with kerosene lamps, built a well,' she reels off, all in one breath, without the faintest pride at the memory.

If there is anything that Vatsalabai does cherish thirty-two years on, it is the perks of being a panchayat member: the jeep that would come to take her to the monthly panchayat meetings in style; the chairs that they sat on at meetings; the photographs, that were taken of them, even the unlikely Americans who came to interview them. 'I'm illiterate. I didn't care. I just put my *angootha chhap* [thumb print] to the papers I was instructed to,' she shrugs. So unaccustomed was Vatsalabai to power of that magnitude, that when it came to her on a platter, she had no idea what to do with it. Likewise with Tarabai Raskar, another *angootha chhap* member, who recalls—without any regret—that their term of office ended when Kamalbai's husband said, *'Aata bas zhala!'* (That's enough now.) And that was that. Kamalbai, whose health had suffered during the panchayat term, was too ill to stand for another election. The other women couldn't imagine standing without her. Thus Babulal's order and Kamalbai's exit effectively brought the shutters down on Nimbut's experiment with women's political empowerment.

Political participation is merely one aspect of women's empowerment. Education is another aspect that many women from the historic 1963 panchayat accord greater emphasis. For Babai Kerba Bansode, a neo-Buddhist member of the 1963 panchayat, education is almost a religion. Babai is a devout follower of social reformer and educationist Babasaheb Ambedkar. Not only are her sons graduates, but one of her daughters, Shobha, insisted on taking her Class XI examination the same day her baby was due. Her guilt-stricken examiners rushed her to the hospital in time, saying, 'Don't worry, we'll pass you.' Shobha's daughter, inspired by the heroine of the television serial *Udaan*, would like to become a gutsy police officer.

Pallavi Hanumant Pharande, 24, granddaughter of another 1963 panchayat member Vatsalabai Dhondiba Pharande, has defied all convention by enrolling in Pune University for an MPhil in economic geography. She is more educationally qualified than any man in the village; she goes around on a bicycle, openly talks to young men in the street, and is clear she will marry a man who has pulled himself up by his bootstraps, not a man of her parents' choice. During my visit, she is busy defending her audacious decision to turn down an eligible man who came to 'see her' a week ago, because he is balding.

MAUJE RUI

Meenakshi Shedde

'Do what you like, so long as you mind the kids.'

Vishwajeet and Shrikant, two village schoolboys from Pune district's Indapur tehsil, are perceptibly different from their classmates. They are articulate, they don't huddle behind the curtains when strangers drop in, and what's more, they take lessons in Taekwondo, a martial art form. If this is because their father is a liberal schoolteacher, it is also because their mother, Padmavati Ramchandra Kare, is bolder than most mothers. Padmavati, a doughty woman from the backward Dhangar (shepherd) caste, initiated the formation of an all-women-panchayat in Indapur tehsil's Mauje Rui village in 1984. 'Mrs Indira Gandhi wrote and it made my mother-in-law proud of me,' says Padmavati, for whom the catalyst for a women's panchayat was the chronic water scarcity in her village of 4,000 people.

'When I went for my SSC examination to Indapur and later to Pune, I saw how different things were for urban women,' says Padmavati. 'And here we were, spending three hours a day making many trips to fetch water from a well half a kilometre away. The men would make sympathetic noises but they wouldn't lift a finger to help us. In two decades of Panchayati Raj, we had just two or three wells. It made me really angry. That's how I came to stand for elections—I knew I'd do better.'

If the immediate catalyst was water scarcity, the broader context was politicization. Padmavati was deeply influenced by her father, a police *patil* or a village policeman who did a great deal for poor people in his village—professionally and personally. Influenced by his example, Padmavati decided to become a lawyer who would fight oppression. Since the village school was only up to the fourth standard, Padmavati walked twenty kilometres daily to a high school in the neighbouring village of Kalas for years, braving the rains without an umbrella.

Another enabling factor was family support. 'I used to make *poli bhaji* (chapati and a vegetable dish), bathe the children, feed and drop them to school,' complains her husband, Ramchandra Kare. 'People were always teasing me, "Oh, the sarpanch's husband! Are the chappatis ready yet?" And my wife would be gone for days at a time when she had to meet the *mamlatdar* at Indapur. Finally I told her, do what you like, so long as you mind the kids.'

Backed by her supportive family, Padmavati started forming her panel. 'Maratha women are not encouraged by their men, so Dhangar women joined me in standing for the elections'. 'The male candidates withdrew, thinking they would seem like hijras if the women defeated them, so we were elected unopposed in 1984.'

The other panchayat members came from liberal families too. The husband of member Radhabai Bhagat had been sarpanch twice earlier, and was chairman of the Rui Cooperative Credit Society. The father of member Sindhu Markad was a village policeman, while her husband was a teacher. For Sindhu, whose son was an electronics engineer in Haryana, 'education is the third eye.'

Even today, Padmavati can proudly rattle off her panchayat's 10-year-old feats. 'By the end of our five-year term we had built one well, which we connected to a tank, fitted pipes, and brought water to our homes. We used to hold classes for children under a tree, or have four or five classes in the same room. We built eight classrooms, and also held adult education classes. Also, we gave credit for afforestation, brought electricity to the Harijan quarter, and built a temple for the Harijans. We have an account of every paisa we spent. My character has been as white as washed rice,' she says, pride lending colour to language.

Why is it then, that as in Nimbut, an all-women panchayat was never elected again? 'The family said that that was enough, and there was a lot of *chirchira* (malicious gossip),' says Sindhu. Padmavati is furious. 'The other women accused me of abandoning my children to become a sarpanch. I asked why they were jealous. What prevented them from becoming sarpanch? As long as I can convince my husband, everybody else can go to hell.'

Despite the gossip, Padmavati continues to participate in local politics. Today, she is one of the two women on the panchayat—and heads the village Mahila Mandal. And in her personal capacity too, Padmavati—like her father—tries to empower women. She has just paid a lawyer out of her own pocket to assist a woman whose husband beat her up and abandoned her. 'I think it is more than my education that has made me the way I am,' she reflects quietly. 'I think I'm just very *ziddi* (obstinate).'

BHENDE KHURD

Bishakha Datta

'That man on the fatfati, he's the sarpanch!'

This tiny village of 1,500 people could teach national politicians a thing or two about skullduggery. Located in Ahmednagar's Newasa taluka, Bhende Khurd's political landscape is dominated by the Dnyaneshwar Cooperative Sugar Factory that towers over the village. Sugarcane is life here. The Dnyaneshwar factory, which has 15,000 farmer members, churns out 3,700 sacks of sugar everyday. For the bigger farmers sugarcane spells riches—one acre produces 65 to 70 tons. At a buying price of Rs 850 per ton, one acre means Rs 50,000. For landless labourers, the crop provides a steady stream of work at Rs 12–15 per day—while the leftover outer husks provide roofing for their mud huts. These days, the cane harvest is at its peak. Carts trundle by carrying cane to the factory whose spires spout endless streams of smoke into a supine sky.

If sugarcane dominates the village economy, it also dominates village politics. Namdeo Rakhmaji Nawle, 49, is one of the village's biggest cane-growers. He is also the most powerful man in the village: from 1965 to 1991, Nawle controlled every single village institution. 'No panchayat elections were held in this village from 1967 to 1992,' says Nawle, proudly. 'Every five years, I was the winner, unopposed.' For 25 years, Nawle held the village in his fist: he was sarpanch, chairman of the Bhende Khurd Development Credit Cooperative Society, founder-secretary at the Dnyaneshwar Sugar Mill, member of the Newasa Taluka Panchayat Samiti, secretary of the district cooperative bank—and member of the Congress Party. What better credentials could an upwardly mobile politician demand?

In Bhende Khurd, political power rests in controlling two local institutions: the development credit society and the panchayat. Two years back, as Nawle lost control of the credit society to another landlord, he hit on a novel way to keep control of the other institution: an all-women panchayat. Although Nawle insists he formed the panchayat after inhaling the heady whiff of women's rights blowing through the government, it is obvious that the nine-women panchayat is nothing but a puppet show. The nine-women body includes three Nawles, two Mapares—members of the Joshi community—and a representative each from the dalit Chambar, Mahar, Nhavi and Wadar communities. This would seem like a smiling snapshot of democracy if the big picture did not lie outside the frame.

In December 1992, right after the panchayat was elected, a generous Nawle treated six women and their husbands to a ten day pilgrimage tour of Maharashtra: Alandi, Pandarpur, Nashik, Trimbakeshwar. As the six holidaying women returned to Bhende—on the day of the sarpanch elections—five meekly agreed to support Nawle's choice for sarpanch. The sixth—Jijabai Mapare—who did not go along with this choice, was offloaded at Shrirampur. By the time she had got to Bhende, the sarpanch was elected 5–3, 1 absent.

Nawle's daughter-in-law, Kusum Vijaykumar Nawle, is sarpanch—or head puppet. Ask anyone where the sarpanch lives: 'The big house, the big house,' they will say. The sarpanch is clearly not one of them; she is 'the woman in the big house'. The villagers refuse to venture into the sarpanch's compound uninvited. What does this say about the panchayat being a representative of the people?

Kusum Nawle is a bit edgy when we visit her; her husband Kumar has gone out and she will have to talk to us alone. Plus, she had planned to visit her three sons, who live and study in an English medium school in Srirampur, two hours from Bhende. Daughter Surekha studies at the Marathi medium school in Bhende. Clearly, English is an aspiration for sons, not daughters. Kusum dials her husband's number restlessly, beseeching him to drop work and come home. 'Visitors have come. Visitors . . .'

What Kusum knows about panchayats could be put on the back of an ant with room to spare. She does not know how many houses there are in a village she heads. She does not know whether any taxes are collected. She does not know anything about Jawahar Rozgar Yojana (JRY) other than its name. She does not know . . . finally, she gets fed up of saying 'I don't know' and waiting for her husband to come and bail her out. 'I'm a woman,' she says. 'Being a woman, I don't know about all this.'

But she does know certain things: the names of the eight other members and their castes; that they came to power in an uncontested election two years back; that panchayat meetings are held for 15–30 minutes each month, 'after all, how much is there for women to discuss?' And Kusum can confidently answer the most damning question of them all: What has your panchayat done so far? They've dug a borewell for water, built a tank, provided two community taps, and built a room for the village primary school.

A borewell. A tank. Two taps. A schoolroom. It looks so good on paper. But the borewell does not work: the motor burnt down months ago and the pumphouse is now overrun with weeds. The tank is dry. The two taps are dry. In Rajwada, the dalit Mahar basti housing 40 families long converted to Christianity, the tap is a joke. 'It's sits there like an idol of Ganpati,' say a group of dalit men and women, gathered nearby. 'But there's no water.'

Water is by far the biggest problem in this village of 1,500 residents. Like other rural staples—land and food—the issue is not one of availability, but one of access. Walk through a sugarcane field. There is enough water around to bathe Bhende's residents 10 times over, but class and caste determine who will get it. Simply put, if you are rich and Maratha, you have your own private well to water your sugarcane fields, your bodies and your family's thirst. If you are poor and dalit, you must go to the landlord's well for water. This innocuous inequity masks a powerful means of social control: if you, dalit labourer, dare to displease the landlord, he will cut off your water supply. Owning a well in a drought-prone area is like owning the only weapon in a war: you are king.

The politics of water is inextricably linked with panchayat politics. The gram panchayat implements the Jawahar Rozgar Yojana at the village level: under a previous grant, two wells were dug in Bhende Khurd. Where were they dug? In the backward-caste *wadas* (colonies) which are desperate for water? No. The panchayat got the wells dug at the houses of Shankar and Anand Dhanawde, relatives of P.D. Dhanawde, current chairman of the Bhende Khurd Development Credit Cooperative Society—and Nawle's biggest political rival.

That these wells were dug at a time when the Maharashtra government's Jeevan Dhara Scheme sanctioned a free motor for each well then dug is not what shocks. What really shocks is the extent of misappropriation: each year's JRY grant is calculated on the basis of a village's population—under JRY, a village gets Rs 42 per backward resident, and Rs 14 per non-backward class resident. Almost 80 percent of Bhende is backward class—which means Bhende gets more under JRY because of the higher allocation for backward class inhabitants. Yet the panchayat felt little compunction in cutting these people—who really comprise a majority—out of the fruits of JRY. The two wells were dug outside the houses of two affluent Maratha families.

While Kusum Nawle washes clothes at her private well, Bhende's poorer women march miles with pots on their heads. A group of women from the dalit Wadar and Rajwadas finally went to sarpanch Kusum's house in the summer of 1993 to ask for water facilities. This unusual bit of courage paid off: the well-pump-tap scheme was built. 'A trickle of salty water came out for two to three days,' say the women at both wadas. 'It couldn't be drunk. Then it stopped.' One year after it stopped, the women feel the water scheme 'was just for show. Just to say "we've done something for you." The women say they still tell the sarpanch about their water problem. 'She keeps saying, "It'll be done. It'll be done." Nothing happens.'

Practically all the 40 families in Rajwada and 100 families in Wadarwada are agricultural labourers. Some own no land. Others own an acre or two. Others have just come home, devastated like Madhukar Kharat by his son's death in a Goregaon chawl during Bombay's 1992 riots. These 140 houses are literally powerless; they tap the overhead power cables and hang naked bulbs in their houses. What does it mean then that sarpanch Kusum has power enough to fuel TV and phone, while her in-laws also boast a fridge and mixer?

Ask the Kharats of Rajwada 'Who is the village sarpanch?' They don't know. 'P. D. Dhanawde,' says one. 'Waman Mapare,' says another. 'Kusum Nawle,' pipes up another. 'But she can't manage, so her husband helps her.' Ask the same question at Wadarwada—they don't know. 'The man on the *fatfati* [mobike]—he's the sarpanch.' 'Pandurang Dhanawde—he has a bungalow; he's the sarpanch.' Is anyone from your wada on the panchayat? 'No no.'

Janabai Dattu Pitekar is actually the panchayat member from Wadarwada. An uneducated landless labourer, she doesn't know when the panchayat started—or who the other members are. 'I don't read or write anything,' she says. 'So why should I go there and sit? If you're educated, you go to meetings. I've never been to one.

Neither has Sindubai Waman Mapare—who believes there are six women on the panchayat. 'They're illiterate,' says husband Waman, whom some villagers mistook for the sarpanch. 'We only look after the work.' The accountant husband of the most educated candidate—Pushpa Nawle—puts it in perspective. 'You won't find anything in this taluka where a decision is made by women; all decisions are made by men.'

In a village where nobody knows who Sindubai Mapare is until you specify she is Sindubai *Waman* Mapare, where is the question of women making decisions for the village? In a village where members confirm no meeting has ever been held, what is the meaning of a panchayat? To a panchayat which has rarely passed on development benefits to the people it claims to represent, what does local self-government mean?

Vinayak Borde has just become the gram sevak of Bhende eight days back. The previous gram sevak was transferred, ostensibly because he was in charge of too many villages. Borde tells us that

i. In Bhende, no houses have ever been built under Indira Awas Yojana, a government scheme meant for providing housing to backward caste people. Every other village we visited has used this scheme,
ii. Next year's JRY grant of Rs 26,000 will be used to build a new gram panchayat office—even though an absentee panchayat is already well-housed in a room in the credit society building,
iii. The village has 100 families living below the poverty line, who are eligible for loans under the Integrated Rural Development Programme (IRDP). We look through the 1982–83 government survey identifying those below the poverty line; it is like standing upside down. The list is *crawling* with Nawles and Dhanawdes, relatives of the two most powerful Maratha families in Bhende; *not even one* Mahar or Kharat figures on the list.

The gram sevak inadvertently confirms that if anyone deserves to be on the list of people below the poverty line—a list that determines access to government IRDP loans—it is the Kharats. He has just drawn up a list of seven backward-class children eligible for the benefits of another welfare scheme: all seven surnames on his list are Kharat.

In Rajwada, the Mahar cluster, where they openly call this a puppet regime, they know that a democratic panchayat cannot root itself in soil that is essentially feudal. That if the Seventy-Third Amendment is an amoeba, Panchayati Raj is its pipedream. 'Rajiv Gandhi came. Narasimha Rao went,' says one man. *'Desh mein kuch badal aaya? Jo Dilli mein, woh gaon mein. Koi badal nahin.'* (Did anything change in the country? As it is in Delhi, so it is here. Absolutely no change.)

RALEGAN SIDDHI

Sonali Sathaye

'Women need to forget their "womanhood".'

Ralegan Siddhi is recognized as a model village of sorts in the world of development. Located in the drought-prone Ahmednagar district, Ralegan was turned into a green oasis of prosperity by social reformer and village patriarch Anna Hazare. Ralegan is well known for its effective watershed management scheme, its use of solar and wind energy, unique schooling system, ethic of *shramdan* (voluntary labour), and its attempt to stop alcoholism. As part of its overall development, an all-women panchayat was also initiated in the village in 1989.

Anna Hazare speaks about the importance of such panchayats:

Why is an all-woman panchayat important ?
Women are very important to a smooth functioning of government and home. They are like one wheel of a chariot, and to function well, a chariot needs both wheels. Right now, women are too burdened with the notion of their womanhood. They need to step out of that, they need to have courage. A panchayat is helpful in allowing them to gain that courage, as it gives them a voice.

How was the panchayat at Ralegan Siddhi formed ?
We had a gram sabha—as we usually do—and I proposed an all-women panchayat. At first nobody spoke up, but slowly one educated woman picked up the courage to do so and came forward. Seeing her, one by one the women started to come forward and soon we had nine.

Was the panchayat effective? Were they able to function independently of you?
Not really. It is only a beginning. These women need support both from their families and the socio-political structure before they can come forward to participate as active citizens

of their society and country. They need to forget their 'womanhood'. As long as they do not do that, they will need help.

Is there a difference between an all-male and an all-women panchayat?
Yes. Given a chance, and if they can overcome their timidity, women can make much better administrators, do more for society. This is because they have not lost their sense of shame. Men have become totally corrupt: they no longer care what people think of them, they have lost their sense of self-respect, which is something women still have.

Do you think there is scope for women's empowerment through the agency of the panchayat, the structure of the panchayat?
Yes, definitely. There is nothing wrong with the centralized nature of the panchayat. Women can easily come to the fore and make a difference to society through this forum—but for this they need a great deal of encouragement from their families as well.
Unfortunately our women have not been able to come forward because of the lack of this sort of encouragement.

NIMBGAON BHOGI

Sonali Sathaye

'I learnt what true politics is about in this village.'

The advent of women in politics—especially in rural India, where women bear a heavy burden of tradition—is generally considered a Good Thing, most fundamentally because it allows women to step out of a world circumscribed by society and claim a share in decision-making. As activists Nandita Shah and Nandita Gandhi write:

> The main reason for encouraging those women who feel like stepping into the political world is . . . that their presence will herald the erosion of one area of the sexual division of labour between men and women in society—men in the outside, public world and women in the private world of the home.[1]

However, women's participation is not considered on par with men's participation either in terms of the method of functioning, or in terms of the aims of government. Socio-cultural notions of the nature of 'woman' typically condition expectations of what a woman's government should be. It is assumed that women are fundamentally somehow 'purer' and less violent than men. Accordingly, governance by women is expected to be more honest, less centralized and more efficient. Activist Lakshmi Krishnamurthy reflects popular perception when she says that 'women with their inherent qualities of organization, capability, and native wisdom would do better in the interest of the public at large'.[2] In the same journal, Revathi Narayanan reports a (female) vice-president of a Zilla Parishad as saying that the 'presence of women members in the panchayat itself leads to more orderly behaviour.'[3]

A related assumption is that when women come to power, their first allegiance will be to women. It is assumed that women will be eager to tackle women's specific problems, to be accessible to women in particular. 'As women experiencing oppression they are likely to have more of an empathy with other women and their problems,' write Nandita Shah and Nandita Gandhi.[4] Increased political participation of women, according to activist Vibhuti Patel, will lead to 'their meaningful contribution in highlighting women-specific issues'.[5]

Although this might be faultless psychological logic, in reality there are numerous factors that determine the direction taken by a woman—or women—in power, other than the one of gender. Personal ambition may play as important a role in the shaping of a woman's government, as the factors of caste, class and family. The election of an all-women panchayat under the leadership of Usha Badhe in Nimbgaon Bhogi village is a case in point.

Nimbgaon Bhogi lies off the main Ahmednagar–Pune highway in Pune district. A two-kilometre stretch of glittering sharp grey stones separates it from the highway. On either side lie yellow-brown fields. A women's panchayat came to power in an unopposed election in Nimbgaon in the summer of 1989. The decision was taken by the elders of the village—all men—in a gram sabha held earlier that year. They had been inspired in the endeavour by Anna Hazare, the ecologically-minded social reformer from the nearby village of Ralegan Siddhi, who had initiated an all-women panchayat in his village that year.

Nimbgaon, a village of 1,000 people, is divided between the wealthy upper-caste Marathas and the lower-caste Malis, who are supported by scheduled caste Mahars, Mangs, Kolis and Dhangars. The post of sarpanch traditionally alternates between these two groups. Usha Badhe, a Maratha graduate in philosophy from Aurangabad University, was nominated sarpanch of the all-women panchayat. The remaining eight seats were divided equally between the Marathas and the coalition of Malis and scheduled castes. Of the nine women, four were literate.

Despite the apparently consensual nature of the election and nomination, four of the women tendered their resignations by the end of the first year. They had earlier registered their protest by passing a no-confidence motion at the end of the first six months. Of the four resignations, only three were accepted to keep the majority. Differing motivations underlying this seemingly 'same' action of resignation bring into focus the complex nature of rural politics. Anjanabai Asavle of the backward Mahar caste is a daily-wage labourer who has studied up to Class V. She resigned, she says, because she was neither informed of panchayat meetings, nor was she consulted in matters of finance dealing with the various schemes. 'If one is not going to be consulted, *tyachya peksha rajinama dilela bara'* (it is better to give in one's resignation).

Ranjana Jadhav cites similar reasons for resigning. Ranjanabai owns three acres of land, but lack of water for irrigation has turned her into a daily-wage worker. *'Bai konacha vicharat naahi'* (the woman doesn't care for anyone), she says of the sarpanch. She is somewhat derisive about the sarpanch visiting the village only once a week, the day her agricultural shop in Shirur is closed. All in all, Ranjanabai says she would prefer a male sarpanch who is present and takes the villagers into account, to a woman who visits occasionally and only does what she pleases.

Yamuna Vyavhare's reasons for resigning appear somewhat less straightforward. Local gossip has it that she was tipped to be the sarpanch instead of Usha Badhe; ultimately she was made deputy sarpanch till she resigned. Educated up to Class VII in her native Pimpalner, Yamunabai has her own political base in Nimbgaon: she is leader of the Mahila Mandal, and has attended several rallies at Nagpur, Pune and Bombay in an official capacity. Both she and her husband are members of the Congress Party.

Political rivalries could have influenced her decision to resign, which the entire family avidly discusses. Her husband, who has reservations about women's rule, is particularly vitriolic in his assessment of 'sarpanchbai,' whom he accuses of running a *'hukumshahicha rajkaran'* (an autocratic regime). It is hard to know how much of this is rooted in fact, how much in the politics of party and gender.

Mrs Raskar provides a soothing contrast to Vyavhare's vitriol. Raskarbai is a toothless old lady who clearly does not know why she resigned—nor why she was elected, for that matter. She says her son came up to her one day and said she must file her papers for panchayat elections. She gave her thumbprint to the papers. In much the same fashion, when he came back to her and said she must resign, she did. Personal relations between her and the sarpanch are still cordial, so that whenever Usha Badhe visits Nimbgaon on her weekly Wednesday visit, she always stops over for a cup of tea at the Raskars.

Although she is the sarpanch, Usha Badhe lives in the taluka headquarters at Shirur, about 10 km from Nimbgaon. The Badhes still retain between 50 to 60 acres of ancestral property in the village. In Shirur too, the Badhes enjoy a comparable measure of affluence. They own the entire building in which they live. Ushatai's brother, a doctor who owns a pathology laboratory and clinic, lives next door, while the ground floor is leased out to the State Bank of India.

Politically, Ushatai is one of those rare women who is acknowledged as a political entity in her own right. She is a member of five committees, including the Panchayat Samiti, the Mahila Mandal which she heads, and the Lok Nyayalaya, literally 'People's Justice' Committee. When asked how one qualifies to be a member of the Lok Nyayalaya, she unabashedly states that all the important members of the town were invited—these include the Block Development Officer (BDO), the police patil, and the collector.

Ushadevi—'devi' (goddess) her husband corrects me, not 'tai' (sister)—is tipped to be the next MLA from the region. Much is made of her 'high connections'—one villager says *'bai khup bhari ahe'* (Bai has heavy clout). He refers to her connections in Shirur's police department, in Pune's state transport corporation, her contacts with influential bureaucrats like the tehsildar and the BDO. Ushadevi herself talks with obvious relish of meetings with the then Members of Parliament Arun Gujarati and Vilasrao Deshmukh. A framed and garlanded photograph of Congress heavyweight Sharad Pawar hangs in the kitchen. The photograph seems of a piece with her perception of politics as a power game. This perception comes through in statements such as *'thodishi aplipan takat dakhvavi, tya shivay aplyala koni manat nahi'* (You have to show your strength if you want to be respected). Ushadevi frequently says she has learnt to be political after becoming sarpanch. *'Khara rajkaran thitech shikle'* (I learnt what true politics is about in Nimbgaon).

Despite Ushadevi's political clout, both she and her husband disclaim all desire for political power. Instead, they claim inspiration from Anna Hazare of Ralegan Siddhi, insisting that they, like him, are in politics for social work. Now and again, Ushadevi also makes a comment about the oppression of women, saying women have the same status as *'naukars'* (servants) all over the country. *'Bai vees gavache netritva pahel, pan ghari navra je mhanel tech karave lagel'* (A woman can manage to look after twenty villages, but at home it is only what her husband says that goes).

Such statements bear little relation to the visible power dynamics between Ushadevi and her husband. I am privy to a fight that breaks out between husband and wife when Ushadevi tries to choose between attending a Panchayat Samiti meeting in Pune and a competing function to address female workers at a factory whose management has asked for her guidance. Ushadevi seems inclined to address the latter, while her husband reminds her that she already has a commitment to the Samiti. Voices are raised and Ushadevi makes constant appeal to me. 'See? This is the state of women everywhere. A wife cannot take a single decision without asking for her husband's permission.' The scene ends with Mr Badhe walking out in a cold fury. I learn from Ushadevi the next morning that she attended the factory function. Later, when I hear stories of how she cannot take a single decision without her husband, the image of a set Ushadevi and a furious—but powerless—Mr Badhe comes to mind.

> *'There has been no water for the fields for more than a year. The rains have been failing Nimbgaon every monsoon for the last four years.'*
>
> Kalavati Raut, deputy sarpanch

> *'Oh, I don't worry about that [the water shortage]. The government will send a tanker when the situation gets desperate.'*
>
> Usha Badhe, sarpanch

Kalabai Sahebrao Raut takes a break from sowing onions in a field that lies on the other side of the highway from Nimbgaon. The onions she has sown today will be ready for harvesting only in five months. Until then, she will get about Rs 20 a day. The total produce of the harvested onions will be worth about Rs 10,000: half will go to the landowners, half will be distributed among all the daily-wage workers. This will leave the Raut family with Rs 5,000, which will have to last them another year at the least. Kalabai has to walk a couple of kilometres under a hot sun every morning to work on someone else's land to make enough.

Today, Kalabai is fearful and anxious of the long dry months ahead when, leave aside water for the fields, even the drinking water is going to disappear. Sarpanch Ushabai agrees with Kalabai; Nimbgaon's biggest problems are water and electricity, she says. But although she claims to have installed a tap in every *basti* settlement to alleviate the village's water problem to some extent, her deputy sarpanch does not know of it.

Ushabai says two borewells have also been dug in the village.

But Anjanabai Asavle who had resigned from being a panchayat member points out that they are still waiting for the handpump that was promised them when the panchayat first came to power. The road that was supposed to enable the transportation of the pump into the interior of Asavle basti—a walk across bumpy furrowed land—has still not been laid down.

Charges of favouritism surround the water supply scheme. The taps Ushabai talks about are rumoured to be only in the Sambare basti, which supports her. The others have to make do with a well built in 1985. I notice no taps in the Jadhav basti when I am in Nimbgaon. There is a similar gap between promises of electricity—and actual delivery. Ushabai says she has asked for 100 electric poles to be installed in the village by the end of the month. The electrification project, which will cost approximately Rs 10 lakhs, will be funded by the Zilla Parishad fund. Although she says 60 of the 100 poles are ready, I find evidence of only about 20 on my visit.

If Ushabai has not been able to meet basic village needs, water and electricity, neither does she see the need to initiate other, new schemes in the village. Asked about beginning a credit-and-savings scheme for the village women, Ushabai answers without a hint of discomfort. '*Khara sangu tar mala velach nahi ahe. Dukan, ghar, ani hya saglya committee var basun kahi velach nahi milat. Mi hi scheme kahi Nimbgaonla nahi annar*' (Frankly, I just don't have the time, what with the shop, the household, and all these committees. No, I am not going to bring this scheme to Nimbgaon).

Little wonder then that villagers see Ushabai as an outsider, with scant regard for village development. Even where villagers concede Ushabai has delivered—for instance, she has extended the school from Class VII to Class X—there are accompanying murmurings of favouritism. The Raskar and Vyavhare bastis buzz with rumours that the school council board is stacked only with Badhe supporters—including 'outsiders' Anna Hazare and her brother. The board also includes her husband, Sahebrao Raut and Mr Phalke, both proven supporters.

Related charges are levelled at Ushabai's interactions with gram sevaks. Nimbgaon has seen seven gram sevaks over the last five years. Although gram panchayat records are in order, people mutter that money from the schemes has disappeared—and that every time a gram sevak disagrees with Ushabai, he is transferred. Oblivious to the veiled charges of favouritism and corruption that surround her, Ushabai continues confidently in her capacity as sarpanch. She says everybody knows that *'kaahi kam asel tar Ushatai kade za'* (if there is work to be done, go to Ushabai.) The sarpanch is equally confident wielding authority. She tells how she hit a drunken, swaying Mr Raskar, sarpanch before her, on a dais in a village gathering as he had threatened to disrupt an adult education scheme.

Ushabai is at pains to assure one of the importance she gives to consensus in the functioning of the panchayat—she did not check the bills after a purchase, she trusted members with money, she says. According to her, the women passed a no-confidence motion against her—and resigned—mainly at the instance of their husbands.

Be that as it may, the women that still remain in the panchayat appear to do so predominantly out of family loyalty. Sahebrao Raut, who risked caste ostracization to support Ushabai during a political crisis, was duly rewarded. His wife, Kalavati, was made deputy sarpanch after four members had resigned. Prabhavati Sambare, daughter-in-law of the village council head, a rich powerful man who owns 30 acres of land, is similarly in the panchayat out of family loyalty. Prabhavati, whose maternal uncle is a Badhe, says her father-in-law insisted that *'aplya gharatun koni pahije'* (there must be someone from our house).

The presence of women like Kalavati—who is illiterate and totally in awe of Ushabai—and Prabhavati—who is clearly a cipher—on the panchayat has only served to give Ushabai a new lease of unlimited power in Nimbgaon. How valid then is Ushabai's assertion of running a consensus government? Having said all this, it must be kept in mind that Ushabai is merely an individual instance of a woman politician who represents her own needs more than those of others. Her case cannot be interpreted to mean that women have no place in politics, that women will bring nothing new to the political arena—or will automatically imitate male political behaviour.

This is the classic trap proffered by Ushabai's most trenchant critic, Krishna Vyavhare. Vyavhare shakes his head and clucks dejectedly about how the women, from whom they expected honesty, have also failed them. *'Aaplyala satta pahije mhanun gavachi ichcha shakti sampavli'* (Because she wanted power, she exhausted our desire and faith in an all-women panchayat).

NOTES

1. Nandita Shah and Nandita Gandhi, *The Quota Question*, Mumbai: Akshara (1991), p.22
2. Lakshmi Krishnamurthy, 'Democracy Seeps Down', *Search News* (Jan-June, 1993), p.29
3. Revathi Narayanan, 'Women in Panchayati Raj—Experiences from Karnataka', *Search News* (Jan-June 1993), p.38
4. 'The Quota Question', op.cit., p.21
5. Vibhuti Patel, 'Getting a Foothold in Politics', Research Centre for Women's Studies, SNDT University, p.2

BRAHMANGHAR

Bishakha Datta

'Instead of having fights between men, let women stand.'

Traditional wisdom has always held the household as the female domain and the world outside as the domain of the male. This thinking is more pronounced in rural areas, where women—even though they work in the fields—are inextricably associated with the kitchen, the inside, the private, while men are linked with the workspace, the outside, the public. 'Women were thought to be incapable of understanding what went on outside the domestic walls,' writes sociologist M. N. Srinivas.[1]

Brahmanghar, a small village of 635 people in Pune district's Bhor taluka, convincingly shatters the 'inside/outside' dichotomy of space. Shubhangi Dhumal gossips with her teenage friends in the *chowdi chowk* or village square, habitually a space reserved for men. Groups of women sit outside their houses, warming themselves in the weak winter sun. Sarpanch Pushpalata Dhumal strides up and down Brahmanghar's main road, calling, cajoling, yelling out to women to come join an impromptu photo-session.

If women have begun to occupy Brahmanghar's public spaces, it is mainly because the men are absent. The picturesque village was resettled here when the Bhatkal Dam swamped its original landholdings in the twenties. But though Brahmanghar sits on the banks of the lake that the dam created, its fields are not irrigated by dam waters. The rain-dependent villagers were forced to grow only one crop of rice each year till they got a loan two years back for a community irrigation scheme. 'There's so little land and the rains sometimes fail,' says Pushpalata Dhumal. 'So the men have to go the city to bring that extra Rs 20 home.'

Pushpalata estimates that 300 men—roughly half the population—have migrated to cities like Mumbai and Pune to secure their livelihoods. This absence of men has inadvertently given Brahmanghar's women access to one layer of male roles and responsibilities. Women not only labour on the field; they also supervise labourers, traditionally a male occupation. Women listen to radios, read newspapers, run credit societies, attend school meetings, and travel alone by bus outside the village. But when it comes to making community decisions, the men are still summoned to the village to take the lead. It was one such summons that resulted in the formation of an all-women panchayat in December 1992, when the Brahmanghar panchayat was finally made independent. (Earlier it formed part of a group panchayat with the neighbouring village of Harnass.) Women were put on the panchayat not because women themselves demanded it, but because the men decided it must be so.

'A necessary precondition for women's mobilization is the general and usually prior mobilization of the men in the rural community,' writes activist Madhu Kishwar. This precondition can be seen quite clearly in Brahmanghar.[2] Influenced by a local Lal Nishan Party (LNP) MLA, the village actively participated in the Samyukta Maharashtra struggle for a unilingual state in the late fifties. Villagers were exposed for the first time to left-wing liberal ideology, an exposure which deepened when Brahmanghar's men participated in the textile mill-workers' struggle in Mumbai.

While these ideologies provided the context for an all-women panchayat, what triggered it off was the need to preserve village unity. Brahmanghar has always been homogenous—socially, economically, and politically—with hardly any tradition of opposition or dissent. All but four of the 110 families living here belong to the same Maratha caste, and share the same surname—Dhumal; there are no Brahmins in Brahmanghar. Practically every family owns the same amount—two to four acres—of land. And the village votes as one entity for the same party during Assembly elections.

'Homogeneity' and 'unity' are so central to Brahmanghar's socio-political identity that external forces like the police, the law or the courts have never been used to settle village disputes. Law and order problems are still arbitrated by elders at the temple. In a village where unity is key, elections—with their attendant factionalism, power struggles, division—were to be avoided at all cost. 'We knew if elections were held there would be a fight,' says village elder Dagdoba Dhumal. Since women are seen neither as political entities nor as having any political aspirations, it was considered safer to elect only women. 'So the men decided, instead of having fights between men, let women stand,' says Shakuntala Gaekwad.

Shakuntala Gaekwad is one of the members of the seven-person panchayat. The Dhumals, the landowning class which comprises the village majority, were given four seats on the panchayat. Other communities, including the backward class Chavans, were given the remaining three seats. Only literate women were chosen: sarpanch Pushpalata Dhumal has studied up to Class VII. Shakuntala Gaekwad has studied up to Class IX and speaks a smattering of English. Even Alka Chavan, visibly the poorest panchayat member, has studied up to Class IV.

All the women are quite clear they would not have entered the political arena without family support. 'Nobody's orthodox in my family,' says Shakuntala Gaekwad. 'But if they hadn't agreed, I wouldn't have come.' Sarpanch Pushpalata Dhumal—who is independent enough to go on pilgrimage alone—echoes this feeling. 'If the men don't cooperate, then what can the women do?' And Alka Chavan says she will only be able to attend an evening panchayat meeting if her husband allows it. 'Tell him to let me off my work,' she says.

But although the women realize that their tryst with politics hinges on male support, they have managed to put their own concerns on the panchayat agenda. Two years back, the panchayat mobilized 22 women to go to the Block Development Officer in Bhor—and demand one more teacher for the village school. 'We said if you don't give us a teacher, we won't budge,' recalls panchayat member Vandana Dhumal. 'The next day the new teacher came to school.' Today the school has four teachers instead of three.

Other panchayat priorities included:

i. constructing additional rooms for two families under the Indira Awas Yojana;
ii. providing toys, slides and swings for the village school;
iii. upgrading a makeshift gutter into a cement and brick gutter which ensures that garbage flows smoothly and doesn't choke up;
iv. starting a subsidized gobar gas scheme which met with only partial success, since each family doesn't have

enough cattle to generate the amount of dung required to make gobar gas.

But the initiative that the women's panchayat is proudest of is the 70-foot road that all the village women built—with voluntary labour—two years back. The road, which runs from the village to the primary school, 'was so narrow that small children couldn't pass,' explains the sarpanch. 'In the rains it was very muddy. Our children used to slip and fall. They could not go.' In March 1993, the sarpanch called a meeting of the village women to discuss the issue. 'We have to do it all ourselves,' she told them. 'We do not have money to spend. Is everybody prepared?' Within two days, the panchayat and the mahila mandal had organized every single village woman—and levied a Rs 25 penalty on each house that didn't send a woman. 'Everyone came,' says Pushpalata. 'Even elderly women, they would sit down and at least put one stone.' Within three days of work, the road was ready.

The resulting sense of achievement is evident even two years later, when the women recreate the scene for a photo-session. The session takes on a life of its own, and before we know it, the schoolyard is spontaneously converted into a women's space, with 50 women singing, dancing, posing, playing *phugdi*, riding on the children's merry-go-round, and generally taking time off from domestic duties.

Two years after this women's panchayat came into existence, it is practically impossible to assess objectively its impact on women's lives. Certainly, exposure to new ideas has ensured that women are better informed on a range of things—and form their own opinions. In addition, a constant flow of visitors and media attention has created a sense of pride. 'My brother came from his village to visit me after reading about it in the papers,' says member Mandakini Dhumal. Their own achievements have indeed convinced them that women count for something. 'Now that one has got this experience,' says Pushpalata, 'one feels the daughter, daughter-in-law, they should also do something.'

But to some extent, the impact that the panchayat has had on women's lives seems to be mediated by their caste and class position. Sarpanch Pushpalata—whose family is one of Brahmanghar's biggest landowners, whose house boasts a television, a gas stove and other symbols of rural affluence—has grown enormously in status. 'Now everywhere it is known that this is an all-women panchayat,' she says. 'So now if we have to get some work done, and we go to the Panchayat Samiti, they give us more attention—because we are all women. So the work gets done faster.'

But from the perspective of the poorest member Alka Chavan, her sudden access to political space has brought few gains to her backward class community. The Chavans have none of the symbols of rural affluence. They don't own rural assets like cows or buffaloes. They cannot afford their share of the village lift-irrigation scheme, so their small plot of land remains unirrigated. There is no milk in the house the day we visit; we are served black tea.

'How has the panchayat benefitted us?' asks Alka Chavan. 'There has been no benefit till today.' Although the panchayat has built an extra room in her house, she feels it hasn't provided other necessities: street lighting for the backward class colony like the rest of the village; water connections in the house; a tar road from the main village road to their colony. She is aware that she doesn't have electricity or a water connection at home because her family cannot afford them. But she still holds the panchayat responsible for this. 'If men came on the panchayat, they would do more work—quicker,' she grumbles.

Alka Chavan's discontent with the women's panchayat is partly born out of frustration at being on a panchayat where her voice is often not heard. Although she says the villagers do not discriminate on the basis of caste, she clearly feels there is little common ground between the upper-caste Dhumals and the backward class Chavans: their problems are different, her problems are different—and her problems get submerged in the bargain. 'I keep telling the sarpanch about the road, electricity,' she says. 'She keeps saying it will be done. But it isn't done.' As a result, she rarely attends panchayat meetings.

But the experience of being on the panchayat and setting village priorities—coupled with the absence of men—has brought with it a nascent women's consciousness. Several panchayat members unequivocally condemn dowry, discuss how tradition has confined women to the kitchen, and talk candidly on subjects like menstruation and infertility. One or two women even talk of the need to transfer a part of the family land in the woman's name. And as part of this process, panchayat members also identify certain problems that are specific to women. 'We haven't done anything for women yet, but we will now,' says Shakuntala

Gaekwad. According to her, the two biggest problems Brahmanghar's women face are the lack of a maternity hospital in the village and the absence of economic schemes that will provide women independent incomes.

'There should be some means of providing steady income to women,' says Shakuntala. 'We have children, the men aren't here, we should have money in our hands. The family depends on us. If her child falls ill, or something happens, the woman needs money.' Like her, many other women stress the need for 'agarbati-making, papad-making, pickle-making' and other schemes which enable the woman to earn at home. A dozen women did enrol for a tailoring scheme last year—and bought subsidized sewing machines. But the scheme flopped as there wasn't enough demand for tailored products in Brahmanghar.

Despite this, the women are slowly taking steps towards economic empowerment. Last year, while going to the Pune Zilla Parishad as part of her panchayat duties, the sarpanch noticed the government savings and credit department nearby. She asked her neighbour, Ranjana Dhumal, to initiate a women's credit society in the village. Less than a year later, the society has 88 women members who save between Rs 20 to Rs 50 each month. 'Every woman has an account,' says Ranjana Dhumal. 'The accounts are in the woman's names. The husband's name is put on the form as heir in case she dies.' What is particularly noteworthy is that this initiative came from Brahmanghar's women, not at the behest of external agencies like NGOs, donors or government departments, which typically initiate savings and credit groups in villages.

But despite the presence of three separate women's groups in the village—panchayat, mahila mandal, credit society—Brahmanghar's women are a long way from participating as equal partners in community decision-making. Women still remain excluded from the village's traditional power bases. Women have no representation on the agricultural credit society which arranged financing for a Rs 14-lakh community irrigation scheme. Women have no voice on the traditional caste panchayat which settles village disputes. And neither do any of the women—in their capacity as water-users and agriculturists—attend the urgent meeting held when the lift-irrigation pipe breaks down. 'But they'll discuss fittings and all,' says Parvati Dhumal. 'Why should we go to the meeting?'

It is clear then that even though women have been allowed to occupy political space, they are still expected to remain in their place.

AFTERWORD

Brahmanghar had elected a woman sarpanch decades before anyone realized the importance of women's political participation. In 1965, Hirabai Karanjavne became sarpanch of the combined panchayat of Brahmanghar and the neighbouring village of Harnass. The village supported her bid for power even though she had walked out of a crumbling marriage and returned to her maternal home. Today Hirabai is a doughty 70 and widely respected as the village matriarch. Her eyesight has faded, her knees hurt, and she walks with a limp. But that doesn't prevent an enthusiastic Hirabai from climbing up to her tiny loft to find and display the letter of congratulation that Indira Gandhi sent her way back then. Here are fragments of what she remembers of her panchayat days:

> 'Working on a group panchayat is worse than living with a *souten* (second wife). . . It's like two women married to the same man.'
>
> 'Even when I was elected in front of everyone, the members from Harnass tried to manipulate the results."She's only a woman, so we'll do some *badmaash* [mischief] and spoil her name." That's what they thought.'
>
> 'Everyone started saying "Hirabai has become sarpanch." But I didn't understand what a sarpanch was. I just didn't know the importance of being a sarpanch.'
>
> 'Then came the time to go to office. All the elders in my family were amazed that a woman is going to work. Older people have different views.
>
> 'At the office, I was given a chair, since I was the sarpanch. "Oh God," I said, "I will not sit on a chair."
>
> 'Indira Gandhi was a woman. How did she manage to run the whole country? Then it is not very difficult for us to do it in the village.'
>
> 'There has been a lot of change since then. Today all the women on the panchayat are educated. During my time, there was no education. If I had to go to Bhor, I couldn't tell where the office was. I couldn't read the signposts. In our times, our brains didn't work so much.'

NOTES

1. M. N. Srinivas, *The Remembered Village*, Delhi : Oxford University Press, (1976), p.141
2. Madhu Kishwar, 'Nature of Women's Mobilization in Rural India', *Economic and Political Weekly* (Dec. 24-31, 1988), p. 2754.

BITARGAON

Sharmila Joshi

'I would like to do this work as long as I live.'

The morning bus to Bitargaon will take you past dry fields of jowar and wheat and other seasonal plants, and drop you off near the village's most prominent landmark: an elevated, concrete water tank. The reservoir is also a milestone in the village's history: since it was built on 30 July 1994, the tank has mitigated Bitargaon's perennial water problem; it has considerably reduced the villagers' dependence on about six handpumps of which only one really worked; it has also halted the daily pre-dawn journeys of the women to the village well.

Diagonally opposite this tank, in a grey brick and stone house, lives Satyabhama Lawand. Till October 1994, Satyabhama—whom the villagers call Nani (imprecisely meaning elder sister)—was sarpanch of Bitargaon. The dry and dusty village of 1,143 people is a half-hour State Transport bus-ride from Kurduwadi, a small town 85 km from Solapur. Nani headed Bitargaon's panchayat of nine uneducated women, which was constituted for five years on 25 October 1989.

The concrete tank was built during Nani's tenure as sarpanch. It is perhaps the most visible symbol in Bitargaon of the all-women panchayat. Since it was built, many of the 139 homes in the village have acquired individual taps that cost between Rs 200 and Rs 300. Perhaps this unprecedented facility will induce the villagers to once again decide to nominate, uncontested, an all-women panchayat for five more years. But a range of other factors must converge as they did in 1989 to form such a panchayat in Bitargaon.

The residents of Bitargaon might never have agreed to an all-women panchayat if male-dominated panels in the past had worked effectively. For several five-year terms, the village had a joint panchayat with Shingewadi, a neighbouring village. 'Since the sarpanch belonged to Shingewadi he worked for that village and there was no improvement in Bitargaon,' says Laxmi

Karande, a member of the all-women panchayat. Bitargaon's two main problems, as perceived by the villagers—the reconstruction of the dilapidated school building and water scarcity—remained unresolved.

It is not clear, from the villagers' accounts, who first started considering alternatives such as an all-women panchayat. The processes could have been simultaneous: of Nani, an exceptionally spirited and articulate woman, believing such a panel would work and trying to convince other women to participate; of the village patriarch Dadasaheb Patil offering his support for the panchayat; and of the village gram sabha endorsing the proposed experiment. The chronology is unclear but these interdependent factors contributed to the eventual formation of the panchayat. However Devidas Patil, one of Dadasaheb's sons, says, 'The basic reason is Nani. It is because of her boldness that all this happened.'

Nani, now possibly in her sixties, had lived a rebellious existence; she was used to taking independent decisions. When her husband died after two years of marriage and the birth of their son, Nani decided to ignore community strictures that barred Maratha women from tilling the land. Not only did Nani yoke the bullocks and plough the land to ensure it was not usurped by her brother-in-law, she also dressed up as a man to go to the grains market at Kurduwadi during harvest time for many years.

Nani had also been a token member of the joint Bitargaon-Shingewadi panchayat for 15 years. She is now a confident village leader, when she entered public life she was relatively diffident. 'I was content with just being made a member, with being called to the office to put my thumbprint on official papers,' she says. By the time the 1989 panchayat elections were announced, Nani was less tied up than in the past with work on her fields and in her home; her son had grown up and she now had a daughter-in-law. The family's finances were also more stable.

So Nani discussed the possibility of an all-women panchayat with other women. 'There were no facilities in the village. Some women felt we could do something about it. We did not like the men's ways of working. And there was no reason to go on accepting their methods. We wanted to get a chance to try.' The women were initially apprehensive and reluctant. 'I started nagging them,' says Nani. 'I told them, enough of being scared. You follow me. I am there with you. Speak when I speak. Let us stand for the elections. Let us see what happens. If any calamity comes, if your mother-in-law or your husband disagrees, I'm there with you.' She told the women, 'Why should only a man roam around and only he do the work? How long must women stay by the fireside? We must now think about bettering our children's lives.'

For six whole months, such discussions went on. Slowly, as a group, the women began to feel some solidarity. 'We had each other's and Nani's support,' says Kamal Mastud, the backward class member. 'Then what was there to be scared of?'

Getting Dadasaheb Patil's support was the next step. Until he died some years ago, Dadasaheb, from all accounts, was a progressive and benign village elder who wielded enormous clout in Bitargaon. He was also informally Nani's adoptive father, and had supported all her unorthodox decisions. His three sons are Bappa Patil, an advocate who lives in Kurduwadi; Devidas Patil, who looks after the family's 200 acres of land and is chairman of the village's Krishi Udyog Society; and Babasaheb Patil, the village policeman. They all continue in their father's influential footsteps. If the Patil clan is not entirely well-meaning, their warts are hidden; the Patils reign as uncontested leaders.

Bitargaon is politically unified; all adult villagers vote for the Congress. Their low level of political awareness increases the villagers' dependence on the Patil family for direction on voting and village development policies. Dadasaheb—who had encouraged Nani to become a member of the previous joint panchayat—has always had a major impact on village politics. When Nani went to him this time too, Dadasaheb said, 'Yes, you can stand. If there is any problem, if anyone crosses paths with you, I am there. You stand fearlessly. I have no objections.' Nani came back and told the women, 'The orders have come. We can move.'

Because of the absence of strident dissent on matters related to public policy, nobody openly objected to the new concept. 'The village decides things together without any opposition,' says Amberao Barangule. 'We decided on an all-women panchayat because they should also be given a chance to advance. Here, some women don't even know how to go to the *kirana* [grain] shop in the village. We thought, how long must we keep them in the dark?'

Once the plan was approved by the all-male gram sabha, Bitargaon officially started nominating women to the panchayat. Avidabai Barde, a frail, restrained woman was nominated sarpanch, more to give her a 'chance', than for any special abilities.

'She had never stepped out of her house,' says Nani. 'She had not moved about here or there or talked with people. We felt she could do it. So we chose her.'

For two years, Avidabai was sarpanch but Nani really led the panchayat. After a while, Avidabai did not want to be sarpanch any longer. 'Then I decided and the women also decided together that I should be sarpanch,' says Nani, who took over formally. The other panchayat members were chosen from 530 village women, according to two criteria: age (40 plus) and total illiteracy. 'I used my discretion to select them,' Nani says. 'How could we appoint someone very old or a very young girl and sit and talk with her? Both wheels should be comparable, only then will the cart run well. The selected ones had to match one another in age, thoughts and behaviour.'

Other than Nani and Avidabai, who continued as member, the women chosen to constitute the panchayat were Kamal Mastud, Laxmi Karande, Nagarbai Kolte, Vatsalabai Parkale, Malan Barangule, Sarubai Mali, and Anusuya Jadhav. It is possible that the family members of the women who formed the panchayat, commented adversely, but privately, on their move. But since the decision was approved by the gram sabha, no husband publicly opposed the candidature of his wife.

'There was no opposition,' says Nagarbai, who thinks she must be 40; she and two women she calls her sisters are married to the same man. Nagarbai could not have children; her husband and 'sisters' have eight. The husband owns, she thinks, 30 acres—though Nagarbai's is among the poorest houses in the village, tiny and *kuchcha*—on which the family grows bajra, tur dal, and corn. 'Nobody questioned how I would go out and work. Nani is knowledgeable. So we stood with her.'

Sarubai Mali, possibly the oldest woman on the panchayat, is a widow with four sons. She will not say her husband's name but asks a grandson to say it. Sarubai's eyesight is failing. 'I liked Nani's work,' she says. 'Because of her I wanted to be on the panchayat.' Similarly, Malan Barangule, a slight, pretty and reticent woman whose family is amongst the wealthiest in the village, says, 'I only stand behind the sarpanch. I feel very scared. The women told me we will support you. So I accepted the nomination.' Malan's family, like the others', did not oppose her move.

Although all the women have tremendous faith in Nani, not all of them have based their decision to participate solely on her support. 'I became a member as one chooses one's desired profession,' says Laxmi Karande, one of the more articulate and informed members. 'There was nothing to be scared about. One had to work according to one's understanding. If something went wrong, that could be rectified.'

Kamal Mastud is the panchayat's sole backward class member. 'I decided to come forward for the reform of our village,' says Kamal, whose much older husband was an alcoholic. 'Not even the children of the village made fun of us. If they tried to say anything, we would say sharply, "What is it to you? We are doing this on our own."'

Bitargaon, which has a majority of Marathas, also has 19 backward class homes that are separately located (as they are in other villages). Although caste relations are not acrimonious, Bitargaon follows certain caste divisions. Till a few years back, says Kamal, the dalits did not draw water from the village well; the Marathas poured it into pitchers for them. Once, she says, members of the Mahar and Mang communities 'forcibly' used the well. Kamal, who is from the Chambhar community, talks of these other backward class families somewhat derisively, as people who 'broke customs'. 'Since then we also started taking the water,' she says.

'But people like us don't go directly into Maratha homes and touch food there,' she adds. 'We may eat sitting next to each other. But even then, we keep our distance. We will wash our own plates. Even if they say don't, should we break the custom? Later they may criticise us.' This fear of criticism also keeps Kamal away from the village temple. 'We prostrate before the God only from a distance. I very much feel like going inside. But one must not break limits. Things should be done amicably, not forcibly.'

The first issue the panchayat addressed—amicably—was the scarcity of water. Mhada taluka has an inadequate canal system; farming depends on a good monsoon. Drought is not uncommon. Even in 1992–93, Bitargaon faced an acute water shortage and had to depend on tankers. Although the village has six borewells, only one functioned. Most of the water was obtained from a distant well. 'Till even a year ago, women had to carry water in pots on their heads,' recalls Mahadev Barde, a farmer. 'From 4 am to 10 am everyday, everyone would be involved in getting water.' The water scarcity, though experienced by all, affected the women the most, since it was their duty to collect and store water. Perhaps this is one reason why previous male-dominated panchayats had not accorded this problem any priority. 'Women would slip and fall carrying the water during the monsoon,' says Nani with indignation. 'Two women even fell into the well. So we said, the village must build a tank first and give us water. Even if there is nothing else in this village we must have water.'

Water scarcity was so severe that, in 1989, Bappa Patil suggested that the panchayat pass a resolution boycotting the next general election if the local member of the Legislative Assembly—whom Patil knows well—did not sign the papers required to sanction the water supply scheme. Bappa is a staunch Congress supporter who would not have liked to antagonize the local party leaders; his idea may have been based on concern for Bitargaon, but it was also a calculated move. 'Immediately, the MLA sort of woke up,' recalls gram sevak Namdeo Mali. 'And he came here.'

At Bitargaon, Nani brought him face to face with the situation. 'When he came, someone said, get water, get tea,' she says. 'I said, no don't give him water, I told him we would have given you tea but there is no water.' The MLA just laughed. 'Then I told him the women fall while fetching water. Men don't have to do it. We need water.' Before leaving, the MLA promised that Bitargaon would get water. 'Then things started moving and immediately, the work was sanctioned,' says Mali.

Two more years passed before any concrete work could begin. In February 1993, the Bitargaon water project comprising pipelines, pumps, standposts, taps and a tank, was started. The cost of Rs 6 lakh was funded equally by the state and central governments. Work on the scheme was frequently delayed. 'The work kept stopping. We were given reasons like the bills have not been paid,' says Nani.

On 30 July 1994, Nani signed a paper which said the contractor had completed his work. She signed on a day when the gram sevak—whom she is totally dependent on for official work since she cannot read or write—was not present. The work, unfortunately, was not over: a motor had not been installed, old pipes had been used in some places, others were leaking, standposts were substandard, the pressure was inadequate. A series of meetings and correspondence ensued. In a few months, the damage was rectified and families in Bitargaon which could immediately afford taps, finally had easy access to water.

The dilapidated school building was next on the women's agenda. 'We had a tin school,' recalls Nani. 'The children would get wet in the monsoon sitting in class and would go home. When the big sahebs came from Solapur, Avidabai [the former sarpanch] said we want a proper one,' says Nani. The gram sevak, as always, drafted the application required to eventually start construction.

In 1993-94 the panchayat used Rs 71,000 from funds received from the Jawahar Rozgar Yojana and a cash prize received from the Maharashtra government as an 'adarsh' (model) tax-collection village to construct four concrete classrooms. Three more rooms are being built.

The school building is now one of the prides of Bitargaon: its outside walls are colourfully painted with maps, landscapes and portraits of national leaders. Classrooms are strewn with educational posters and streamers left over from past celebrations. The school holds classes up to Class VII for 86 boys and 74 girls, taught by eight male teachers. Bitargaon would like to have a high school up to Class X but government rules say it is ineligible, since a high school exists just 2 km away.

The school and the water supply scheme are functional necessities. But the television set and the telephone are the 'luxuries' the panchayat is most proud of acquiring. 'As soon as I stood, we asked for a television for the village,' says former sarpanch Avidabai. In all conversations about the panchayat, she always mentions the television set, perhaps because it is perceived as a visible status symbol. Both the television and the telephone—apparently used for making STD calls to relatives—are kept in the panchayat office. But hardly any women watch television (when they do, they sit at the back; men and children sit in front). And no woman, not even Nani, has ever used the phone.

One of the more interesting aspects of the Bitargaon panchayat is its adoption of a portfolio system, which the gram sevak says is mandatory for panchayats in Maharashtra. The Bitargaon panchayat has five portfolios; construction, education, health, prohibition and miscellaneous. But most of the women merely thumbprint official documents related to the portfolio, put before them by the gram sevak.

'I headed the construction portfolio,' says Avidabai. She is reminded that she was only a member of the construction subcommittee. 'Is that so? Maybe I headed something else. I can't remember.' Nagarbai, who actually headed the construction portfolio, says she sometimes supervised road repairs but is unaware who liaised with contractors; she doesn't know how, when or by whom the water tank was built.

Kamal Mastud says she chose the prohibition portfolio because her husband was a severe drinker. She has two daughters and two sons, who, she says, are truck drivers in Bombay. The Mastuds own less than an acre of land on which they grow (or try to—the outcome of all sowing in water-scarce Bitargaon is speculative) chilli and cotton.

The panchayat decided that any man who came drunk to the village—Bitargaon has no liquor shops—would be fined Rs 100. But Kamal did not ever have to actually ask for a fine. The announcement of such a fine, claim the villagers, was a strong enough deterrent. And Nani was an even stronger deterrent. 'Men knew that women were on the panchayat and if they drank, Nani would come to their homes,' says Kamal.

According to Kamal, even her own husband does not come drunk here since they became panchayat members. Her husband recalls a time when he drank and beat his wife—she went and told the panchayat women. 'All nine came to my house. For three days I did not get food,' he says. But this incident is not verified by the others.

Laxmi Karande, 35, was given the health portfolio. One of her sons is a teacher; her daughter, like all Bitargaon's girls, was sent to school only till Class VII; she was married a few years later. The Karandes own 25 acres of land, on which they grow jowar, sunflower and wheat. The family seems well off—Laxmi is the only woman who offers us coffee, regarded as a luxury in the village. Previous panchayats, she says, limited their health activities to purifying (disinfecting) the well on special occasions like the *palkhi* (a religious fair), and distributing anti-malaria tablets once a month. Laxmi says she has tried to improve health facilities. In addition to the responsibilities mentioned above, she ensures that gutters are kept clean—and sends Digamber Khadgale, the sepoy, during emergencies to call the government doctor or nurse. In reality, there have been few emergencies. But Laxmi does at least seem aware of what managing a health portfolio entails. 'I found out for myself what my duties were. Nobody explained it to me.'

Villagers in Bitargaon regard a local dispensary as one of their most critical unmet needs. 'For five years we have been asking for a dispensary,' Laxmi says. 'But our proposal has been rejected.' This is because Bitargaon is less than 5 km from the nearest dispensary. The women's panchayat organizes regular fortnightly visits by a government mobile dispensary to vaccinate children, check pregnant women and give medicines. A local resident Dr Barangule, who practised outside, has moved back to Bitargaon. His move is not connected to the panchayat. But with his arrival and the van's visits, there are fewer health-related problems, according to Laxmi. 'That is why we feel like doing this work.'

It is unlikely that the members of the all-women panchayat could have done the work they did without the help of the competent Namdeo Mali. Mali, who has been gram sevak of Bitargaon since 1988, conducts monthly panchayat meetings, pursues every proposal, does the paperwork, and ensures that projects are implemented. Mali's input is critical—since none of the panchayat members can read or write. In fact, he functions almost as a low-key de facto sarpanch.

Unless there is a complaint against a gram sevak, he—all gram sevaks are male government employees—stays in a village for at least five years; at times he may stay longer, like Mali did for 12 years in Akalkot. 'A gram sevak's life is full of *dhoka*,' (cheating), says the dhoti-clad, intelligent- looking Mali, who is about 50. 'Because in the gram sevak's hands, are the strings of progress. Often gram sevaks take bribes. But you can ask anyone if I have ever asked.' In Bitargaon, it is hardly necessary to ask about Mali's credentials. At a panchayat meeting, Mali reads out his minutes of the meeting and asks, 'Is anything incorrect?' Nani replies, 'Nothing. If anything is wrong you will take care of it.' There is more substantial evidence of Mali's allegiance to Bitargaon: in a dispute over the water supply scheme, he took the village's side—not that of the state government, which employs him.

It is mandatory for every gram panchayat to meet at least once a month. When the date and time for a meeting are fixed by Nani and Bhausaheb (the villagers' name for Mali), Diga (as the villagers call the sepoy) is sent on his bicycle through village lanes and fields to inform panchayat members. Registers show that members attend meetings regularly even though they may not always speak at them. We attended the meeting of June 1994. Although the women's participation at this meeting is not invisible, the meeting—and therefore the direction of the panchayat's work—is entirely led by Mali. But he says the women are very powerful, that nothing can be done without their sanction.

Seven women were present at this meeting at the gram panchayat office; two—Kamal and Avidabai—could not come. The meeting started at 10.30 a.m.; the women had to drop farm-work to be able to attend. The women thumbprint their presence on a register. The sarpanch slowly, painstakingly signs her name (she learnt this in an adult literacy class held in Bitargaon soon after the panchayat was started). The gram sevak presides over four registers and six rubber stamps. As he puts on his glasses to read out the minutes of the previous 29 May meeting, Nani tells him, 'Get us through all this paperwork, two things: school up to Class X and a dispensary.'

The gram sevak talks about expenses to be sanctioned for street lights and stationery. The subject is discussed, with Laxmi, Vatsalabai and even Malan asking a question each. The discussion veers to the amount to be spent on backward class students, and the inequities of being rich and poor is brought up. 'If all were to be rich, then who will be poor?' philosophizes one woman.

The panchayat must decide whether to spend money on slates and books for backward class students, or on uniforms. Each woman has at least one comment.

'Since one uniform would cost Rs 100 at least, Rs 1,000 is not enough for 32 students.'

'The expenditure must be equal for all.'

'We must provide that which is not available at home.'

No one thinks of asking the backward families what they need. Mali reads out his recording of the agreed expenditure; everyone agrees that it is OK. But even if it were not, would any of the women have objected on her own?

Despite five years of an all-women panchayat, villagers still see politics as a male domain. This is evident from the gram sabha. A village must, according to government stipulations, hold a gram sabha—a meeting of the village electorate (voters)—at least twice a year. Bitargaon calls a sabha on 26 January and on 15 August. The gram sabha we attended on 15 August 1994, was practically a men-only event. No woman was present as the national flag was hoisted and the anthem sung. Women peeped out from the corners of buildings to see what was happening in their absence. Some of the panchayat women came later. Even Nani—who was coaxed to speak at the sabha—said she was there for the first time.

Villagers clearly don't feel an all-male sabha is an anomaly in a village with an all-women panchayat. This is evident from the following talk with the otherwise progressive Mali:

'Who attends the gram sabha?' we ask.
'Everyone,' he says.
'Everyone?'
'Yes, everyone.'
'Do the men attend?' we specify.
'Yes.'
'The women?'
'No, no.'

Clearly 'everyone' in this context means 'men', even though women—as voters—theoretically enjoy equal representation on the gram sabha. However, Nani insists that gram sabha decisions do not dictate the gram panchayat's agenda. 'We've told them that whatever we do, we do as per the rules. No one is to speak. If they like it, well and good. But even otherwise, what we do must be accepted.'

One coincidental factor that has unwittingly helped the women's panchayat was the introduction of the Jawahar Rozgar Yojana (JRY) in 1989. JRY—which is the major source of panchayat funds—sanctions funds according to village population: Rs 42 per backward class family and Rs 14 per non-backward class family. In its first year, Bitargaon received Rs 41,000 under the JRY. Previous panchayats had access only to less generous schemes: the Indira Awas Yojana and the National Rural Employment Programme (NREP), with which two women's toilet blocks were built here. Today they are in total disuse: they lack plumbing and the women find them dirty.

Mali believes personality clashes between members also made the old panchayats less effective. 'Now, it is different,' he says. 'Since all are women, no one opposes. They propose, pass a resolution. The men would oppose.' Male panchayat members would also be more confident and experienced in village politics and therefore in a position to oppose.

'We work as *"ek jeev"* [one],' says Kamal, 'What work did they do? There were so many complaints. No water, no school, nothing.' Malan also says, 'Can any work they did be seen here?' Partly because of this lack of any tangible development—in turn induced by a lack of funds—the fairly routine work done by the women's panchayat stands out in contrast as substantial.

The work the all-women panchayat did—a water tank, school renovation, road repairs, and so on—is much the kind of work neighbouring villages (with male-dominated panchayats) have done during the same period. In nearby Tembhurna village in the last five years, a panchayat office was built, roads and handpumps were repaired, rooms were added to the existing school, and in 1993 the village acquired a primary health centre. In neighbouring Mitkalwadi too, a male-dominated panchayat brought electricity and better roads, repaired handpumps and completed a tapwater project. Again, this is partly due to the homogeneity of development brought about by JRY, whose use is primarily sanctioned—by the Panchayat Samiti which must approve all JRY expenditures—for construction.

Is there then, any real difference between an all-women panchayat and a male-dominated panchayat in terms of what the council can achieve? Kamal Mastud believes there is. She says that because the women faced a severe water problem, 'we completed the tapwater scheme. Men would not have done the kind of work we did.'

She doesn't believe that a mixed panchayat would have given priority to the school: 'What is the need of a school? If not here, they would send their children elsewhere. But girls cannot go to other villages to study. Small children have to be accompanied by women. How does all this affect men?' Mali is in complete agreement. 'Who suffers the most in bringing water? In cooking at home?' he asks. 'The women contributed to the development of this village. If the women don't have a share in power, development will not take place. It is like the two wheels of a vehicle. If one wheel is not working properly, the other wheel cannot move forward.'

Despite their involvement in local politics for five years, the women seem to have gained little—in terms of political knowledge, or an understanding of the panchayati system. Most of them—including Nani to some extent—are not aware of how much money the panchayat receives each month and what schemes are available to the village.

'We informed ourselves about what work needs to be done. Why do we need any other information?' asks Kamal, who is still not aware that Bitargaon had a panchayat before theirs was formed. 'There must have been something,' she says. 'Someone, maybe a man.'

When discussing a relative of Avidabai, who is on the panchayat samiti, Nani says, 'She has to go to Kurduwadi to—what do you call it [the panchayat samiti]? I do not know, I don't know anything about that.' Says Laxmi: 'I only know about going to the panchayat office for meetings, and that we must do this or that. I've never stepped out of Bitargaon for any panchayat work.' The only time the women, with the exception of Nani, have been outside Bitargaon on official work is when they visited the taluka headquarter, Mhada, to sign their nomination forms. But many have no idea what they signed.

The women are equally unaware of elections and political parties. The entire village votes for a Congress candidate who is close to Bappa Patil. 'Whatever difficulty we have, we go and meet him and he takes care of our problems,' says Nani. Adds Malan: 'I gave my vote to the hand [Congress] because all the village does so and for no other reason.' Apart from Nani, no one can recall the local MLA's name. The only familiar name is that of Indira Gandhi. Nani often uses Indira Gandhi as an example of her ideal leader ('Look at how she roamed the world, and look at our women toiling in the fields and at home.')

'We only get to know about what happens in neighbouring villages,' Nani says, 'Like when a father and son are both in politics. One lane votes for the father, another lane votes for the son. Father wins and son loses. Then one gets murdered. We hear such things. We also keep a watch on what is happening in the world, which village is going what way, where people are happy. We knew about the Killari earthquake because of the television.' Nani says she has tried to make other women understand something of what she knows. 'It is our job to make them understand. If there is a small child going towards dirt it is our job to pick it up. Slowly, I have brought the women out. It's my duty to explain and to tell them to improve. I have made them move ahead, little by little. My authority was such, no one ever said anything to me. So I took them out slowly, made them move about, to the office, to meetings, to attend, to discuss.'

Although panchayat members understand that water scarcity affects women the most, a similar consciousness does not inform their understanding of wider women's issues. Dowry, for instance, is widely prevalent in Bitargaon. 'It happens in every house in the village during every wedding,' says Nani. The women on the panchayat do not comprehend that such issues are of special significance to them. Nani is surprised when asked why panchayat members have not discussed dowry, even in informal situations. 'How can one do that? It is a hidden thing, secretive,' she says. 'How can we talk about it? Is it like a purchase deed in the taluka office? It's done in the houses without an open word. Then how can we prevent it?'

Later however, after we discuss the subject, she agrees it might be a good idea for the panchayat women to talk about such issues. But Nani also believes a gram panchayat must strictly follow official procedures, and only take up issues according to a predetermined agenda, issues which can produce tangible results. She does not feel the panchayat is a forum to discuss broader issues that are harder to resolve.

Second marriages by men are not uncommon in Bitargaon. Panchayat member Nagarbai's husband married two women after she couldn't conceive. Laxmi also sees nothing wrong in such marriages. 'If a man does not have an offspring then we must help him with a second marriage,' she says, This indicates her belief that it is a wife's duty to produce children. 'He should also take care of the first wife though and not desert her,' she adds.

The one women's issue that the panchayat women feel strongly about is women's education. During different conversations, all of them mention that lack of education has been a huge hurdle in their lives. 'We have two eyes,' says Nani. 'The educated have two and a half.' In its first year, the panchayat had started an adult literacy class where only Nani learnt to sign her name; the classes ceased because women stopped attending after a while.

'I could not go because of work in the fields,' says Kamal, who stays near her land, far from the village centre. Avidabai adds that whenever women walked to the evening classes, they were teased by children. 'They would take away our slates, they would shout. If we started writing something, they would take away our pencils.' Nani, however, questions such excuses. 'Do village women really want to learn?' she asks. They would say our fingers cannot move now (we cannot learn to write) and then even I stopped studying anymore.'

Education is an area where villagers draw a clear dividing line between boys and girls. 'There were no schools for girls in our time,' says Nani. 'Even if there were, who in those days would have sent girls in villages to schools? In our time boys were put in school, girls were put to the cattle.' But although the women themselves perceive the need for education—and talk about the need to extend the village school to Class X—they will not send their daughters to study after Class VII in schools in other villages. 'How can we send girls outside the village?' asks even the better informed Laxmi. 'We are afraid to send grown-up girls to other villages,' says Nagarbai. None of the women are able to articulate what they are afraid of. Only Nani says they've heard stories of boys throwing stones at some girls in some unknown village; Bitargaon has had no such direct experience. 'But the fear is there, always in the mind. If four or five girls went together, there might be no fear.'

Poverty also forces parents to send sons, rather than daughters, to high school. Daughters get married by about the age of 16 in Bitargaon. If a girl is going to be married a few years after completing Class VII, what is the use of that education? we ask Nani. She has an immediate answer: the more educated a girl is in Bitargaon, the less the dowry required for her. Women like Nani express the difference between the sexes in rich, earthy terms. 'A son is like a lamp being lit; a daughter darkness falling.' 'A girl is the shade of a tamarind tree, a boy is that of a mango tree. Because of the boy, the family expands.' But the daughter too has her role. 'A girl is needed to weep, to cry when we die, saying "Oh, my mother died, my mother died." A daughter weeps and makes the whole village weep. But a son never weeps. He simply hangs down his head. There's a difference between their love. That's why a daughter should be there.'

The personal options which opened up for the women on the panchayat are less tangible than the concrete water tank. From an outsider's perspective, nothing much seems to have changed in terms of the women's status over the last five years. But seen with their own points of reference, the benefits have been significant. 'The women got so much power,' explains Nani, 'power so that people obeyed them. The fact that people respected what they said and did pleased the women. That no one drinks now, there is less trouble—that much power, that much comfort in the hearts. That the villagers feel they ought to follow her decisions, that much satisfaction. Earlier, the husbands would never talk gently, now they talk with a little concern. All this means we are more content now.'

Perhaps the biggest indicator of contentment is that many of the women—notably Malan and Laxmi—say they would like to stand for another term; the panchayat was dissolved on 27 October 1994. Kamal is satisfied with their previous term in office. 'We earned a good name and we feel good about that.' Nani adds that with some experience, they know how some things work. 'And once you know something you feel less fear. Now, if the women sit and talk or go somewhere, since there is no criticism or condemnation, there is also no fear.' Malan expresses it differently. 'Because of the panchayat, we at least get that much time to sit and talk about things, otherwise everyday we had to do the same work, at home and in the fields.'

For Nani, the experience has been even more special. 'I feel good,' she says, 'that the women gave me so much of *maya* [affection]. They listened to me. If a husband says come to the field they might say no, but if I'd say come to the office they would never refuse. Eight women from eight houses listened to me more than they listened to their mother-in-law. They gave respect to my word. I would like to do this work as long as I live. But even if we don't stand for another five years, this experience will have been enough.'

INTERVIEW WITH SATYABHAMA 'NANI' LAWAND

'A big gunny bag can be lifted only if all come together. Can I do it just by myself?'

Q: Earlier women were all intimidated by men, who didn't allow them to work. You told [the women] that [we] shouldn't be suppressed like this. So what exactly did you say? Tell us.

A: First, let me tell you how I came out, how I became independent, how I sat among men of achievements. My parents wedded me to a man as his second wife—that is after his first wife was dead.

Q: Why did they do that?

A: Because there was land, social position, a big family. Things were hard in my father's large family. My in-laws were better off. Even in times of drought, a girl would get to eat at least vegetables there. Two years after my marriage, my husband died. He was ill, there was no dispensary in those days. My son was one year old then.

Q: What was wrong with your husband?

A: He had a temperature. What did I know? I didn't know him too well. In those days there wasn't enough familiarity, nothing. Those were different days—now it's different. There wasn't any conversation between us. He was at Talegaon, but I wasn't allowed to go and meet him or see how ill he was or inquire if he was feeling better.

Q: Who prevented you?

A: My brother-in-law. My husband's brother would go to meet him, give him medicine. I would only be in the fields. There was a servant appointed by my husband, so I was to get the farming done, water the fields and so on. I had to get things done by the servant. Then my husband was brought home in a cart. He died during harvest time, at *shimaga*. Our festival. My husband had given his land to his own brothers on rent. My brothers-in-law were not giving it back to me, but I kept it nevertheless.

Q: How did you keep it all by yourself?

A: They said, among us a lone woman can't farm the land. [You] shouldn't keep a servant. I said, I will. Fate has decreed this *vanvas* to me, now I want to till the land. My son is young today, but one day he will be grown up. He will ask me, what did you do then? If I stay at my parents', he may not get educated, the land may not remain with us. Then there's the tiller's land act. Because of the fear that the land might go to the tenants, I didn't go to my parents. I stayed here. I had no support from my brother-in-law, only from my Patilbhau.

Q: Who is this Patilbhau?

A: Bappa's father. He supported me.

Q: But how did you, a lone woman, dare do all this?

A: Because I had the daring and there was Patilbhau to support me. I said now I'm a daughter of this village. My father also said, she is your daughter. My daughter is dead. Now you save her or kill her, I'm not going to take her to my place. When I gave her in marriage, she died for me. Now you do the cremation. Then Patilbhau took my responsibility. To guard, to see if anyone says anything. . . At times I would go, take the bullocks, go to the farm and yoke them. Not to be afraid at all, Patilbhau had told me. My brother-in-law had told me not to keep a young servant but only an old one. I said the work cannot be managed even by this one; how will an older one do it? I want to appoint this one only. Like this I behaved with guts. I said, I won't sit among women, I'll sit among the men. I won't sit [at home] in the evenings.

Q: How did you learn this?

A: Independently. Since the day my father gave me to an old man with three children—yes, he had three children—since then it was my desire to stand on my own. . . I'll do and show them. People said, she won't stay. My brother-in-law said [our women] don't go to shops and markets. They don't go to the well. [I said] I will go to the well, to Kurduwadi, to offices, to Mhada. If I do two things wrong, chop me with a sword. It's my father's name at stake. Do you lose anything? Like this we quarrelled: 'Don't go to shop', 'I will'; 'Don't go to the market', 'I will'.

If I had come away, would the land have remained for my child? Then I took back my land which was given on rent, appointed a servant, and following his steps, I myself toiled in the land. With no one's support, nothing. Except Patilbhau to explain to me what to do.

Later, I bought 20 acres of land at Mhada from the money I earned by tilling my husband's land. Twenty acres of land at Warkute. Then after that I bought some land of Barde, five acres. I had to go to the Talathi's office to get it done.

Q: How did you learn all these jobs related to farming?

A: Learnt it at my father's place. To till the land. There he had lots of farming land. There was water, three-four wells, seven uncles, educated brothers. I used that information here.

Q: But to go to the Talathi's office and write those things. . . how did you learn that?

A: Independently. I would always question the Talathi. He would ask for money or a thumb impression, so I would ask what it was for. I would warn him! See, take care, what are you taking it for. Otherwise my land might go, I have a young child. And if you cheat me, take my thumb impression, then I will take away your job. Then the people sitting around would say, Don't worry Nani, go ahead and give the impression. Then I would do it. Thus I moved about and became bold.

Q: But were you afraid in the beginning?

A: No, never. There was no reason to be afraid. Since my husband died, I had never once been scared. I consider this one as brother, that one as sister. There was so much to do. Who would do them when all I had was a one year old child.

Q: What was your age then?

A: (Counts) 15, 16, 17. . . All this I did since the age of 18. Since then, the entire responsibility came to me. For the house, for the fields, for Kurduwadi, for Mhada, for everything. Then of course I moved about everywhere. I became bold, never found a reason to be scared. It is inborn. I used to wear a dhoti and people with me, like my brother-in-law, used to think that the one doing the farming was a man; not a woman. The woman was sleeping at home and a man was working. Like this I've worked.

Q: You actually did so ?

A: Yes, wearing such a dress.

Q: You really did so? Or simply thought of doing so?

A: I did it actually.

Q: What did you do?

A: Various farming jobs like holding *dhar* (watering) yoking the cart, taking it to Kurduwadi and back, carrying money with me. . . all this I did wearing a dhoti so that people thought that that was a man; not a woman. Like this I worked. When Kurduwadi neared I would wrap a dhoti round me and in a man's voice yell at the bullocks. Call out like a man, not like a woman (mimics).

Q: It's very difficult to believe.

A: In a man's voice I would say 'Run Putalya, Maitya run!' Like this.

Q: All alone or along with your child?

A: All alone. My child was young, he was at school. How was he to know all this? Even today he doesn't know this, even today.

Q: But why did you dress like a man while going out?

A: But isn't it the custom among us that women shouldn't do such jobs. People criticize if a woman goes to water [the fields], or to the market, said my brother-in-law. If she goes to an office or to a shop. That wasn't the custom among us either. In the house of my brother-in-law or in my maternal home. But, if I had been cowed down would my son have come up to here? Or would farming have been possible? Or would this construction have been possible?

No, it is not just my credit, it is all due to God. But if one acts, only then things happen. Can these things happen if we don't do them? First one must work, then only will the fruits appear. People of this village were all like brother and sister to me, no one ever winked at me, touched me or made an indecent gesture. To everyone I was Nani. For everyone, I'm Nani, be it a small child or an old man, I'm Nani.

Q: When you used to dress up like a man, no one ever recognized that you were not a man but a woman? No one?

A: No. Never. They used to come back.

Q: What do you mean ?

A: People used to come back from the woods to check whether Nani was sleeping at home or was in the woods. Then they would say Nani was at home.

Q: But no one realized?

A: No. Even now if I dress up like a man, they don't recognize me. This Patil who was talking here, I could deceive him too. Dressed up like a man, I've eaten *paan* with him, dined in his company, even then he didn't recognize me.

Q: How many years passed till you got your land back from your brother-in-law?

A: This I got before my son's marriage. That is before 1972, I got my land. When it was with him, I worked as a labourer. I went to dig the soil. . . For two years on five annas a day. I got two girls married. Two girls of my husband's first wife.

Q: They used to stay with you? You brought them up?

A: Yes. I brought them up, I got them married.

Q: And their mother?

A: She died when they were young. Then I came out of such a vanvas and today I'm sitting here. I've gone through a lot. So much. Sometimes I didn't have water to wash my head, and no food for two or three days. Through such vanvas, I've come up and I'm sitting now among people, with dignity. First I wasn't as able as this.

Q: You've really done a lot.

A: Ten acres of land, a mill, this building which cost 70 thousand, I did it all on my own.

Q: You've really done a great job. But when you decided to have an all-women panchayat, you gathered all the other women. They mustn't have been so courageous then?

A: Then I nagged these women. Enough of this fear. I'm there with you. You follow me. Speak where I speak. Agree to a thing when I say 'yes'. We will stand for the election. Let's see what happens, who says what! See, later you may be cowed down. 'What will my husband say, what will my mother-in-law say?' You may get scared, but you should not, at all. If any calamity comes, I'm there, if there is no calamity even then I'm there. But you should always come behind me. They agreed. 'If you're there Nani, we're totally with you.' Then I approached Patilbhau, and put before him the proposal. 'Bhau I wish to enter politics. If you give your wholehearted permission, then we will stand.' He said, 'If you have the daring, do it'. If you want to stand, you want to be sarpanch, then we've nothing to say.' No one else wanted to be [sarpanch]. All of us were together. No one speaks before Bhau.

Q: But even before this you've worked in the gram panchayat, didn't you?

A: Fifteen years. As a member. Group panchayat. I was in it for 15 years.

Q: What work did you do there? There must have been men as well?

A: Yes, there were men. They would do everything. Why would I ask for anything there? I would simply go and sign.

Q: Then how did you come to participate in it?

A: Bhau made me stand for that panchayat. Old Bhau told me to stand at that time. 'You do talk, you're bold. People tremble to speak. When you're there, women will have courage, there will be reform.'

Q: You also wanted to be part of it?

A: Very much. When I got Bhau's permission, I became fully active. Everyone was happy. Old people as well as children. There wasn't any jealousy, or bad feelings about me in anyone's heart, or bad looks. No, never. From the beginning.

Q: But how did you make the women understand?

A: I told them not to remain under pressure, we should get information, find out what is going on in the world. We must know what is going on in the world. Leave behind the old ways. We should think of the betterment of our sons, daughters-in-law, and of their children. Can't we even get to understand what and how things are done in the world? Why won't it be done if we do it? What can be done by me? A big gunny bag can be lifted only if all come together. Can I do it just by myself? Whatever is, is of God Pandurang. He gave me wisdom, knowledge, he supported me throughout. I haven't done anything. He turned my earthen things to gold.

Q: Why do you think women usually remain suppressed?

A: Because they have no information. They don't even know how to buy four annas of cumin seeds. They only go on toiling in the fields. Do they know anything beyond that? Any knowledge of the world, what things are required to be done. Do they know anything of this? Their husbands bring things home, they know how to make *bhaji-bhakari* (vegetables and chapati) and serve them, that is all they know. Where do they go inquiring in the village, in the office, in the market, purchasing things? They know nothing. . . won't they remain suppressed?

Q: By whom ?

A: Say, by the husband, by the house, by the world. But we shouldn't remain under pressure. Why should we? We eat of our own making. Why should I be scared of you?

Q: But why did you want to have only women in the panchayat?

A: The men have done most things till today. They move around a lot, go here and there. Can't we do the same? If we can't, then we ask them how to keep accounts and so on. We had adamantly decided not to take them then. What for? Do they teach us anything properly? Thus, we didn't keep any contact with them whatsoever. These men have addictions, pay bribes, eat up money, destroy work; then they come up with excuses. Here work wasn't done, this didn't happen, that couldn't happen. Who is going to ask them anything? Can a woman do so? They would say, 'Do you know anything? Do you understand anything?' Why should we compromise? Their way is very annoying and different. So are their intentions. We saw no reason to take them. We decided our own members and decided to work by ourselves.

Q: In the beginning did any man oppose or laugh at you?

A: No, no one. The acceptance was total, you see. There was firework to celebrate.

Q: After the panchayat was formed what was the first work you took up?

A: Our first work? Was it of the office? The first school? The one which we showed you. Another one is being constructed. Also the office. Yes, four schools. Yes, drainage as well.

Q : Who decided that the beginning should be made with the school?

A : We ourselves decided. Do the children have a school? They used to get soaked. Then the school was closed. Then their studies suffered. If it got cloudy, they would go early.

Q : Why did you give so much importance to the school? You had a shortage of water as well.

A : See, the importance of education is growing. Either the dowry is more, or the education is more. If the girl is educated, then the boy approves, if the boy is educated then the girl approves. They inquire whether the person is educated. Then shouldn't we provide for the school?

Q : What were you saying about dowry?

A : Is the girl educated or is there dowry, they ask. What should the person without money do then? The girl should at least be educated. We can say our daughter is educated.

Q : If the girl is educated, dowry is less.

A : Yes, a little less is required to be given.

Q : Is the custom of dowry very strong in this area?

A : One lakh, 50, 55, 70, 80, 90.

Q : So much?

A : So much! From where can we get it? Do we have good fertile land?

Q : Then have you women thought anything about dowry?

A: How can we do that? Dowry is a hidden thing. Secretive. How can we think about it? Let it come out in the open. We will put them immediately behind bars. If they do it openly we will say it is dowry. But how do we know of it when it's given silently?

Q : But what do you think about dowry?

A : We feel dowry shouldn't be there. It should be stopped.

Q : But it won't?

A : How will it? It's a hidden thing. Is it like a purchase deed done in the taluka?

Q : If education is so important, why won't you send a girl outside the village to learn after the Class VIII?

A : We're scared. Boys may throw stones at them. Do some mischief.

Q : So what if they throw stones? Why are you scared?

A : Yes, we are. Girls get scared. There's always a difference between a village and a city. A village is a village. They have knowledge of no kind. In cities it's different. They have knowledge there. . . education is knowledge. What have we got here?

Q : What exactly is the fear behind not sending the girls? What can happen which makes them scared?

A : See, it's a village. The atmosphere is different. Sending the girls is a risk. All kinds of things might be said, they might be stopped on the way. Boys in villages block the roads.

Q : But can't you tell a few things to the boys?

A : Can you stop a boy by telling? How can you later say which boy it was? When you send the girls outside, if they come back when it's late or if it's raining, then can the girl remember who the boy was and from which village? Who is to be named and with whom to quarrel when it's outside the village?

Q : But does it happen often?

A : No, it doesn't. But the fear is there in the villages. Always. In the mind itself.

Q : Even if she's uneducated, she'll get married at the age of 17. Then what's the importance of education?

A : Should I tell you the importance of education? Now if one woman learns, others also want to, and if she gets a job other women also want to, and if she goes out then I also should go, that's how today's girls feel.

Q : But if the girl gets married after Class X will her house allow her to work?

A: Where is she going to get a job so easily?

Q : Suppose she gets some small job?

A : Then it is up to her husband.

Q : Isn't her wish important?

A : If she wishes, but her husband doesn't allow, what then? Some husbands even let her learn first and then allow her to work. But that's a thing of later times. Suppose we start with the Class X girl andshe says, I don't want to marry, I want to go to Class XI, XII and then do a course; in such case if the girl is good in studies, the parents wait, they don't marry her off.

Q : But why can't the girl decide for herself if she wants to work? Why must she obtain the husband's permission?

A : See it's the parents' mistake to marry her off in a hurry. Parents are responsible for the daughter's loss. They teach her upto Class X, don't send her to school after that. Even if she wishes they say no. The girl cries miserably, no, I don't want marriage, I want to learn. They say, no, sending a girl outside for education is not good. Where to put her up, where will she stay? The world is not good. This way of education is not good and so on. Later if the husband wishes so, he allows her to learn. If not, she sits before the *choolha* making *bhakaris*.

Q: Then don't you women discuss this?

A: If there is no girl educated up to Class X, what is the use of discussing?

Q: Hasn't even one girl passed her Class X?

A: Oh a girl did. But if there's no school, why discuss it? If it is there then only we will say let her do her Class X, don't marry her off. But if the girl is at home only after Class VII then how to discuss it?
Now the only wish is to let the girls go up to Class X. Then the dowry will also come down; and even if it doesn't, when a girl is educated it is reflected in her house, family. In her behaviour. Because she is not educated, she eats humble pie. That's my only wish : to have a school upto Class X.

Q: But even if a girl learns upto Class X or Class XII and gets married, she can't decide for herself whether to work or not. Why is the permission of her husband required?

A: If the husband says my wife is not to work, then what do we do?

Q: But it's her life.

A: Yes.

Q: Then why does he take the decisions?

A: Because she goes into his hands, into his control, when she gets married to him.

Q: Doesn't she have a right over her own life?

A: No, no. It's not allowed, not in the villages, however one may say. That's how it is in the villages. Once married, it is his right. We may say let our daughter work, he says no my wife shouldn't. We lose our right over her.

Q: Do you think you should do something about the fact that she cannot exercise her rights, and her life is not in her hands?

A: I feel, I should but what can be done? And how?

Q: May be just discussions in the beginning, as even now no one discusses these topics. . .

A: Now I'll discuss how we do not have the right, to be self-dependent, how we do not get education. I'll hold discussions next time.But in the villages people are ignorant, I tell you. There should be knowledge. Our Marathwada has remained backward because of this lack of knowledge, they never think of self-dependence or education, or improvement or about the difference between men and women, that's for certain.

Q: You're not educated, even then you have done so much. You showed so much boldness. If you were educated, do you think it would have made a difference?

A: There would've been bright light. Education is so important. Earlier I had only two eyes.

Q: Even then you did so much.

A: That's with my head. It makes the difference. Things happen if you act. We should show them by doing something. If they say don't use the plough, then use it.

Q: Your husband is no more. But when the other women started working in the panchayat, did any change take place in their houses?

A: No, nothing changed. No mother-in-law or father-in-law or husband said any bad words. If you have to go somewhere or if you are called, then you go; if not then you work in the fields, or in the house. No one said anything.

Q: But was there any change or at least a thought like, now that women are working outside, in the panchayat, so some husbands could work in the house?

A: Husbands doing housework?

Q: Yes, why don't they?

A: Husbands and housework?

Q: Yes, now that women work outside.

A: There are other people in the house, they take over when we go out.

Q: But don't you think husbands should? A woman does look after the housework as well as outside work.

A: No, we can't say. Our men won't be able to. These modern, educated boys do. But from the earlier generation, they won't sweep with a broom or cook or won't do anything in the house, they will come, dine and go. They won't think of cooking because the woman has gone out.

Q: What do you think of that?

A : Nothing.
Q: Do people in the village still want only sons?
A : Some people do wish to have a daughter. After four sons they say now we will have a daughter and then we will go for the operation. My own sister waited and waited to have a daughter. After getting four sons, finally she underwent an operation thinking if she took further chance she might get another son.
Q : After having sons, why do they want to have a daughter?
A : A girl is needed to weep, to bring her back home for Diwali.
Q : She is required for weeping? What do you mean?
A : To cry when we die, to weep saying, 'O, my mother has died, my mother has died.' A daughter cries, and makes the village cry. A son never cries, he doesn't get it. He simply hangs down his head. There's a difference between their love, therefore a daughter should be there. A daughter has more affection for her parents. And she makes the entire society weep and feel the loss.
Q : Why can't the sons weep?
A : They do not get tears. They weep but only in a low voice. That's the difference between their love. Girls have more affection. She goes out, she leaves the house, she has no right here. Yet the difference is there.
Q : So for these reasons; to weep and for festivals a daughter is wanted. What does she do in festivals?
A : What does she do? She comes at the time of Diwali, she graces the festival. At Panchami time she goes to dance, we give her bangles, some money, a saree and some gifts. The festival is complete with her presence. A son should be there as a lamp, a creeper plant. There is expansion when a son is there.
Q : What is the meaning of 'expansion'?
A : He gets married, gets children, as the creeper grows. The girl goes out, if there is no son, what remains? Nothing. The house is locked and deserted. Who will be there? The daughter goes away, then who remains? A boy is the light of the family.
Q : Does it mean that a girl is like darkness?
A : Darkness. A girl is like the shade of a tamarind tree, a boy is like that of a mango tree. Mango is sweet and tamarind is sour. And because of the boy the family expands.

Q : But do you agree with these thoughts and beliefs about a girl and a boy?

A : Yes, I do.

Q : But don't you think that these belittle a girl? Seeing the girl as an outsider, a tamarind tree and so on? What does she lack for her to be considered of less importance?

A : She belongs to others, she is not ours.

Q : Why doesn't she have anything of her own?

A: She doesn't have anything. Who is going to give her any land or property?

Q : I know she is not given any property, but why so? What's the reason?

A : It's been like that from the beginning. If from the beginning it had been that the girl gets two acres and the boy gets two acres, then it would have continued like that even today. But custom has always had it the other way round.

Q : Do you think it should be changed?

A : How does it matter how I feel it or how you feel? The entire system should change. If the raj changes, all will change.

Q : But do you feel that it should change?

A : If I alone feel that, will they agree?

Q : Whether it's accepted or not is another thing.

A : Then, yes. A girl and a boy are the same. Both are born from our womb, they are the same, we should treat them equally. At least if two portions are given to him, one could be given to the girl. At least a quarter should be there for the girl.

Q : Are such things—for instance that the girl should have a right over land, rights of a woman, that she is in no way less, that she is also a human being like a man and so on—are these things ever discussed among you or in the panchayat?

A : This topic should never be kept on the agenda. When we discuss, it is about work which should be done. What's the point of just discussing and talking?

Q : Because it's not likely to happen, it shouldn't be discussed?

A : Yes, since it won't happen, it should not be discussed. If we say something, then the words should be respected.

Q : Isn't there any point in discussion? Shouldn't things just be discussed?

A : No, we don't wish to.

Q : See, you're the sarpanch, you do a lot of work. Your case is different. But the rest of them, do you think that because they've become members of the panchayat they have got more power. Take the case of Mastudbai, the chamar, what power did she get?

A: She got a little power.

Q: Over what?

A: About liquor.

Q: But later no one did anything. So what power did she really get?

A: Power means that the people obeyed. The fact that people respect what she says pleases her. No one drinks now, there is no trouble. That is power. Comfort to her heart that no one drinks. That much power. That much satisfaction in her mind. That the villagers feel they ought to obey her. That the power is in a woman's hands, they have to listen to her.

Q: Now that you're the sarpanch, what according to you should your commitment to the village be? Or to the women? Or to yourself?

A: Not to myself. It should be for the good of the village, of the poor, and for the betterment of women. Women should be informed about various things. They should be told that unless they move about, mix with people, they won't know how things are, how the atmosphere is. Let them say anything behind our backs, or criticize us, we should walk ahead. We shouldn't retreat.

Q: But have you and other members of the gram panchayat done anything about the issues pertaining to women, like say women's rights over land, or their health problems?

A: Not so far.

Q: Are there any more problems for the women?

A: No, nothing more.

Q: Just as there are difficulties for the women similarly there are difficulties for the dalits. They have less land and some of them have no land at all. Has the gram panchayat ever discussed this issue?

A: We discuss the poor people. As I told you before, the children of these backward classes, their clothes, sending them to school, fees and so on, all this requires attention.

Q: Do you ever discuss whether the poor should have land in their name?

A: Indira Gandhi had made the law that if you have ten acres, five acres are to be given to the poor. The ceiling was there, wasn't it? But it failed, otherwise poverty would have been demolished, isn't it?

Q: Then why don't you do it like that? Why don't you transfer the land in the poor people's name who don't have land?

A: Will it be legal? Such a law should be there.

Q: Will the people do it then?

A: If it's legal. If such a law comes, automatically you will have two acres, she'll have one acre, I'll have three acres, then things will be according to the law for sure.

Q: But do the people in the gram panchayat realize that this is not right, that the poor don't have any land while we have so much, so something should be done about this? Do they discuss these things?

A: How will such a discussion take place? No, it won't. Does it mean that we only do something for their good? We do give clothes etc. Only if such a rule or law comes that Nani, give two acres of yours, and one of yours, then people will have to obey it.
It should be according to the law.

Q: Suppose there is a law, then will people give willingly or with a grudge?

A: Why with a grudge? No.

Q: Will they think, why should we give them ours?

A: No. Nothing like that. A rule is a rule. When there is a rule, everyone gives in.

Q: Then why wait for a law to be enacted? This is good work, why not do it ourselves? Why wait for rules?

A: No, they won't give without a law. Who will? They won't give even vegetables, wheat or onion or brinjal. Land is such a thing that even while giving to your own child, you hesitate. Among brothers as well. To the poor they will give only if a law comes, but this won't be discussed.

Q: What improvement has all this brought about, in the thinking of the women? They're still so scared.

A: They think on their own, get some concessions in the house, have more information about the house, about money, about people and the world, or about their husbands also, or what happened by being with Nani. This satisfaction now they have earlier there was suppression. 'Do this, do that, fill the bucket, go to the woods, come soon.' Husbands who would never talk gently, now talk a little gently, with concern.

'Where do you have to go today, do you have a meeting today?' Women are more content now.

Q: How come the husbands have started talking with concern?

A: Because the women have come out. Now this Nani has taken these women out, now Nani wishes to let them go. How long will the women remain under your pressure? Now they've come out. Now they cannot be denied their rights. Now they cannot be told 'No'.

Part II

Maiah Wankhede, sarpanch of
Metikheda's all-women panchayat

INTRODUCTION

'Now the gram panchayat will become a kitchen and a cowshed.'

The following report is based primarily on the writings of activists Gail Omvedt and Chetna Galla. Details are given in the notes.

SHETKARI SANGHATANA

In 1985, when the Shetkari Sanghatana decided to take up the issue of rural women's exclusion from political power, its leader was accused of turning from a 'pragmatist' into a 'romantic'. 'The notion of women making a bid for actual political power was at this point rather outside the imagination of most of the other forces in the state,' writes sociologist and activist Gail Omvedt.[1]

Why did the Shetkari Sanghatana—a Maharashtra-based peasant movement that lobbied mainly for remunerative agricultural prices—take up the issue of women's political participation? To understand this, it is necessary to understand the Sanghatana's political philosophy, the nature of participation of peasant women in the movement, and the movement's larger decision to take up women's issues, of which women's political representation is one aspect. All these factors ultimately led to the spontaneous formation of five Sanghatana-backed all-women panchayats in Maharashtra from 1989 to 1994.

When the Shetkari Sanghatana spilt out of a 1979 protest of onion-growing farmers in Nasik and Pune, women's issues were nowhere on its agenda. Omvedt locates the Sanghatana's politics in the rise of the 'new peasant movement' that swept through India's middle peasantry in the late seventies:

> The new peasant movement is based not among tenants fighting against landlords and moneylenders, or among agricultural labourers fighting 'landlords' or 'kulak' farmers, or among hill and forest-dwelling adivasi peasants fighting against an oppressive State, but mainly among middle peasants in areas of intensified commodity production and fighting on issues dealing with their exploitation

via the market, from opposition to raises in electricity and water rates, to movements for higher prices for their crops.[2]

The new peasant movement typically manifested itself in the formation of regional parties that represented its interests—the Rajya Raitha Sangha in Karnataka and Tikait's Bharatiya Kisan Union are two of the best known. In Maharashtra, the Shetkari Sanghatana took up the demands of the middle peasantry with the slogan, 'We don't want alms but the reward for our sweat.'[3]

Sharad Joshi, an International Postal Workers' Union official turned agricultural activist, provided much of the intellectual leadership for the formation of the Sanghatana. Joshi rooted the movement's political philosophy in the gulf between a privileged, urban, industrialized 'India' and an underprivileged, rural, agricultural 'Bharat'—whose interests the Sanghatana represented. Sanghatana activist Chetna Galla describes the divide thus:

> India has its base in centralized industry, and includes industrialists, high-ranking bureaucrats, well-paid salaried employees in the cities, and landlords, politicians of sugar cooperatives and village-level *dadas* (thugs) in the countryside. Bharat includes peasants, artisans, even small traders, unorganized sector workers of all kinds, even in the cities, pavement dwellers, all of those who have been impoverished and marginalized with centralized industrial development and the terms of trade going against agriculture. With this very broad line of division and under the slogan of remunerative prices for agriculture, rural Maharashtra got organized.[4]

SHETKARI SANGHATANA AND WOMEN'S ISSUES

In an essay exploring rural women's mobilization, activist Madhu Kishwar writes that Sharad Joshi did not initially think of drawing women into the organization. 'However, from very early on, women would spontaneously come out in large numbers for mass actions such as *rasta rokos*. It was through this experience that the leadership slowly became aware of the potential that women represented.' According to Kishwar, the participation of women brought with it a new militancy into the movement. She cites an anecdote recounted by Joshi to support her thesis. During the 1980 onion agitation, everyone was startled when an old woman stood up and said she wanted to speak at a public meeting in Nasik. Addressing the men, she said, 'If men don't want to join the agitation, we offer them our bangles to wear and sit at home. We women have decided to join the agitation anyway.'[5]

If this was a turning point for the movement, perhaps it also brought the Sanghatana to a tentative understanding that women could be seen as a specific political group, with specific needs, interests and priorities. This understanding of the specificity of women's oppression is spelt out in *Striyancha Prashna: Chandwad-chi Shidori* (The Women's Question), a booklet that the Sanghatana handed out at its historic Chandwad gathering in November 1986. Omvedt writes that the booklet clearly stated that 'the general solution of peasant problems will not automatically solve the problems of the women of their families, and that the women of "India" (urban, middle-class or whatever) are also oppressed'.[6]

If internal processes impelled the Sanghatana to start thinking on the women's question, external dynamics also played their role. The growing women's movement in Maharashtra provided the larger context, within which Sanghatana leaders drew parallels between women's oppression and peasant oppression. 'The idea that women were not rewarded for their household labour is similar to the idea of unrewarded peasant labour,' writes Galla.[7] Omvedt, however, reports Sharad Joshi's own striking reasoning for taking up women's issues: 'Peasants. . . are in the end only a section and cannot be a national political force, but women can be!'[8]

In 1985, the Sanghatana decided to organize a women's conference. Four preparatory three-day camps were held in different parts of Maharashtra. Kishwar recounts a Sanghatana activist's description of how difficult it was initially to get women to talk about their problems. 'When Joshi asked the women to express their problems, they went on talking only about unremunerative prices. Finally, Joshi said, "Look, leave all these questions of prices and agricultural produce to us men. What problems do you have as women?"'

It took another whole day of talk about government policy before a desperate Joshi finally asked the women to answer only the questions he asked. 'There was only Sharad Bhayya and a couple of other men in the hall and about 150 women. The doors were closed and the loudspeaker removed. He said: "Forget that anyone is listening and say what is in your hearts." In a little while, everyone started telling her problem—someone's husband used to beat her, someone's husband was a drunkard, someone's husband refused to let her have any say in financial affairs of the house. Many women started crying.'[9]

Sanghatana activist and Metikheda sarpanch Maiah Wankhede still remembers the unique atmosphere at those camps. Joshi insisted that 'those who wear nine-yard sarees should talk more,' says Maiah. 'because wearing a five-yard saree means you are progressive and have suffered less.' Men were roped in to serve the women lunch. 'They fed us first and whatever remained, the male members used to eat all that.' The women talked of a range of issues, Maiah recalls—divorce, desertion, even the class divide among women. One old woman stood up and showed her scratched legs at the meeting. 'Look at my legs,' she said. 'You say all women are equal, but here I came walking all the way 15 km, barefoot, and here are these ladies walking with slippers on the carpet!' As talk flew thick and fast, a core group of women was constituted to isolate important issues to go into the historic 1986 Chandwad resolution.[10]

CHANDWAD AND WOMEN'S POLITICAL PARTICIPATION

'The small taluka town of Chandwad, on a drought-hammered plateau beneath the imposing Deccan cliffs, was the scene on 9–10 November of what may have been the biggest women's meeting, certainly the biggest rural women's meeting in Indian history,' writes Omvedt.[11] Sanghatana members typically assemble every 10 November to commemorate the death of farmers in a police firing; in 1986, that day took on a deeper shade of meaning. It is hard to estimate how many women attended the meeting. Omvedt estimates that 5,000–8,000 women attended as delegates while 25,000 women and 100,000 men attended the open sessions. Other observers and journalists talk in figures of lakhs; 200,000 women seems to be a figure commonly agreed on.

'The significance of the Chandwad gathering, however, lay not only in its numbers, but also in the radical nature of many of the positions taken,' writes Omvedt.[12] The meeting resolved to view 'development from a women's perspective', a resolution which ultimately led to the formation of the movement's Samagra Mahila Aghadi (All-Women Front). Two of the most radical resolutions drafted were on securing property rights for women—and ensuring rural women's political participation.

The resolution located the rationale for women's political participation in the understanding that women are the worst victims of the growing degradation, centralization and *goondaism* (thuggery) that are part and parcel of mainstream politics. It read thus:

> With a view to breaking the impasse, all women in Maharashtra should unite to secure power up to the district level, and with this end in view, all women's organizations should come together and present a unified list of women candidates in the forthcoming (zilla parishad and panchayat samiti) elections.[13]

Even before Chandwad, the issue of women's political participation had received some sporadic attention. Omvedt reports that a series of seminars for rural women throughout Maharashtra had been held in 1982–84 at V. M. Dandekar's School for Political Economy in Lonavla. At these seminars, 'women talked of the bossism and corruption in the village governing institutions, asking why they themselves could not be sarpanches or sit in gram panchayats.'[14] Even though women's organizations in the state had yet to grapple with this issue, individual women were grappling with it at the grassroots. Usha Nikam, a freedom fighter from Satara district, had put up a women's panel for gram panchayat elections in her village Indoli in 1984. A similar panel had been put up in Palshi taluka of Satara district. The Sanghatana had not played a role in either of these.

The beauty of the Chandwad resolution was simply that it drew these individual strands together into institutional policy. For the first time in rural Maharashtra, a non-political mass movement called for women to contest panchayat elections. It needs to be emphasised here that the Sanghatana had remained determinedly non-political thus far. Sanghatana activists were not allowed to contest elections. Galla says there had been constant pressure from activists to take part in politics. 'The leadership was opposed to it, saw it as dangerous for the organization, but some form of political expression seemed to be needed.' This may have informed the decision to allow women to participate in politics. 'It was said that due to their particular oppression, women would be excused from the normal Sanghatana ban on electoral participation.'[15]

Be that as it may, how did people react to this declaration? There were ambivalent reactions: murmurs of women being 'used,' and of Joshi turning into a romantic. Several women's organizations chose to stay away from this association; others joined in. In the Sanghatana too, there was some initial resistance. It was said that suitable women candidates could not be found. Women reported their husbands as saying 'put up other women, but don't you stand.' Others argued that only 50 percent of seats should be contested by women. Some women themselves expressed doubts, while others felt that in fighting for political power, they were 'making history.' But all reservations were brushed aside once Sharad Joshi reiterated his commitment to the stated plan of action.

Sanghatana activists believe that the most significant reaction to their decision to field women candidates was the 1990 decision of the then Maharashtra chief minister Sharad Pawar to reserve 30 percent of seats in local bodies (zilla parishads and municipalities) for women. Interestingly, the Sanghatana opposed reservations for women: 'If the women can win 100 percent of the seats on their own, why do we need 30 percent reservation?'

SHETKARI SANGHATANA AND ALL-WOMEN PANCHAYATS

The decision to field all-women panels for the gram panchayat elections of 1989 emanated not from the leadership of the Sanghatana, but as a spontaneous initiative from village-based Sanghatana activists who had participated in the discussions on women's political participation. 'Women's panels were not a Sanghatana policy at this [the village] level,' writes Omvedt.[16] Five villages in four districts set up Sanghatana-backed all-women panels. Four of these were elected in toto; one is a mostly-women panel with two male members. The panchayats are all located in Vidarbha's cotton and orange belt, a Sanghatana stronghold since its early days. The four all-women panchayats are at Metikheda in Yavatmal district, Vitner in Jalgaon district, Yenora in Wardha district, and Salod in Amravati district. At Erangaon in Amravati district, the presence of two men technically makes this a mostly-women panchayat.

Metikheda and Vitner have possibly seen the widest 'effective' participation by women in panchayat politics—and have recorded tremendous gains from this process. At the same time, the dynamics, modes of participation and opposition in both these villages are entirely different. Thus Metikheda and Vitner are discussed in detail in the following two chapters. The other three panchayats are discussed briefly.

YENORA

In Wardha district's Yenora, the women's panel had been formed at the behest of Vasant Borde, a doctor and Sanghatana MLA, whose ancestral home is in Yenora. Despite his support, the nine-women panchayat got off to a rocky start in 1989. Galla writes that the previous panchayat stripped the office bare when they left, removing tables and chairs and leaving behind a pot of dung. 'Why do women need chairs and tables to sit on?' they asked. 'Now the gram panchayat will become a kitchen and cowshed.'[17] There could be no better indicator of the barriers raised by the traditional notion of 'a woman's place'.

There are other indicators that the nine elected women, all dalits, remained incidental to the process of political participation. Sarpanch Ujwala Gote's name could not be recalled at the time of filing nominations; she was mistakenly identified as Karuna Gote. Even though only women members attend panchayat meetings, villagers totally bypassed the panchayat—and directly approached Borde, the MLA, to solve their water problems. Borde, who owns 70 acres of land in Yenora, sanctioned money for a water pipeline from a MLA fund.

The women claim credit for other visibles: a road built from the MLA's house to village interiors; two classrooms that shifted the school from its earlier location in someone's courtyard; tin roofs provided under the Samaj Kalyan Scheme; and subsidies provided to people below the poverty line. A community toilet for women and income-generation schemes have yet to be sanctioned. But perhaps the real experience of being on the panchayat is voiced by members Aruna Raut and Satyabhama Borde. 'At the meetings, we nod our heads. When we come home, we forget everything.'

SALOD

This pattern of participation—or lack of it—is replicated in Salod in Amravati district, where a Muslim woman headed an all-women panchayat from 1989-94. Sarpanch Sairabi Sattar is a docile woman who has studied up to Class III (daughter Muniza explains that girls stop studying at menstruation) and is content to fade into the background, letting her husband speak for her. The Sattars own no land, but hire out their cattle for farmwork to earn a living. Other women from the nine-member panchayat confirm that meetings are rarely held—when they are, their husbands attend. The panchayat registers have not been filled since 1992; many women have no idea why a women's panchayat was formed. Sairabi herself feels it is unnecessary for women to attend panchayat meetings. *'Ab jab shohar hai, to biwi ko kya zaroorat hai waha jaane ka?'* (When the husband is there, what is the need for the wife to attend the meeting?)

ERANGAON

Erangaon, just an hour's autorickshaw ride from Salod in Amravati district, presents a prettier picture of women's political participation. Seven out of nine panchayat members are women; the other two members are men from an opposing panel backed by the Shiv Sena.

Sarpanch Anjanabai Toras is a hardy 55-year-old woman who has a bad cough when we visit. Anjanabai, who studied up to Class III, married at twelve and now has five sons. Her husband owns 42 acres of land; oranges and sacks of groundnuts lie around the house. Anjanabai explains that her panchayat built a school block, sewerage *nullahs*, a cattleshed, and 10–15 gobar gas plants, of which only two or three still work. She explains that liquor is a major problem; 117 women had signed a petition demanding that liquor breweries be shut down.

Motiram Malwe, one of the two male members, owns three acres of land. He makes his displeasure at working with women quite clear. 'I would prefer not to work under the panel than work under them.' Malwe's awareness of panchayat workings and schemes—Jeevan Dhara, JRY, bank loans—is a sharp contrast to the women's knowledge of such schemes. The sarpanch has vaguely heard of JRY, but has never heard of Jeevan Dhara. Other panchayat members—Gitabai Wankhede and Tulsabai Gabhane—have no idea of such things. They do not even know that their panchayat term is over! Despite all this, Sanghatana activist Sapan Modghare is quite clear of his expectations of a women's panchayat. 'A little bird has to learn to fly on its own. The mother will give it food, but at one point, the mother pushes it away, makes it fly on its own. In a similar way, the Shetkari Sanghatana has nursed the mahila panchayat. Even if they have not done anything in five years, it doesn't matter.'

These panchayats were set up in the late eighties, when the Sanghatana broke a ten year policy against electoral positions and formally entered the political arena. In 1990, for the first time, the movement fielded 35 candidates for the State Assembly elections (on Janata Dal tickets). 10 of these—an unprecedented 28 percent—were women.[18]

Today, the Sanghatana has become a full-fledged entrant into the political arena. Sharad Joshi's party, Swatantra Bharat, contested all 288 seats in the 1995 Maharashtra Assembly elections. But despite its larger focus on politics, the issue of women's participation in Panchayati Raj seems to have receded from its agenda. In stark contrast to the 1989 elections, not a single all-women panel was fielded during the 1995 gram panchayat elections.

NOTES

1. Gail Omvedt, 'The Farmers' Movement in Maharastra', in Ilina Sen, ed., *A Space Within the Struggle* (Delhi: Kali for Women, 1990), p.243
2. ibid, 235
3. Chetna Galla, 'The Empowerment of Women—The Shetkari Sanghatana's Experience in Maharashtra', (Unpublished report) p.1
4. ibid, 2
5. Madhu Kishwar, 'Nature of Women's Mobilisation in Rural India', *Economic and Political Weekly*, (24-31 Dec 1988), p.2754, p.2756
6. Gail Omvedt, 'Peasants and Women—Challenge of Chadwad', *Economic and Political Weekly*, (29 Nov 1986), p.2085
7. Galla , 'Empowerment of Women'
8. Omvedt, 'Peasants and Women', p.2085,
9. Kishwar, 'Nature of Women's Mobilisation', p.2758
10. Maiah Wankhede, personal taped interview, (May 1995)
11. Omvedt, 'Peasants and Women', p.2085
12. Omvedt, 'The Farmers' Movement in Maharastra', p.238
13. ibid
14. ibid, 241
15. Galla, 'Empowerment of Women'
16. Gail Omvedt, 'Women, Zilla Parishads and Panchayat Raj', *Economic and Political Weekly* (4 August 1990) p.1687
17. Galla, 'Empowerment of Woman'
18. Omvedt, 'Women, Zilla Parishads and Panchayati Raj', p.1689.

METIKHEDA

Bishakha Datta

'The amount of work the ladies did, the men will not do.'

May is the slack season in Metikheda, a dry month of dull brown light, parched riverbeds and no work. A group of men sit on a hillock and discuss village politics. 'The work that the women's panchayat did has not been done for 40 years,' says Ankush Khadse, lolling on a *charpoy*. On the other side of the village, the same topic is raising hackles of heat. 'These women have done no work in five years, and they want to be re-elected,' asks Vijay Saroday. 'Why? '

Both these opinions should be digested with a pinch of salt; Khadse and Saroday are rivals in the gram panchayat elections of May 1995. Khadse heads the Shetkari Sanghatana-backed Gao Panel, a coalition of dalits, adivasis, women and landless labourers that brought an all-women panchayat to power here in 1989. Saroday heads what the Gao Panel scornfully dubs the Rao Panel, with its attendant implications of top-down Congress political culture. According to the Gao panel, the Rao panel is a dud. Ostensibly stacked with landless labourers who work on the 125-acre Saroday farm, its real goal, they say, is to regain Vijay Saroday's vicelike grip on the gram panchayat—and to continue the powerful Saroday family's 30-year domination of Metikheda's political institutions.

Who will win? No one knows: gram panchayat candidates often win by margins as tiny as 20 votes! Candidates walk around the village, reminding voters to stamp the right symbol. Party symbols are disallowed in gram panchayat elections which are contested by non-party panels. The Gao panel has opted for a tiger, a clock, and a moon for its nine candidates (there are three election wards in Metikheda; three candidates stand from each ward). The Rao panel goes by an umbrella, a man and a mango.

But even if national political symbols are absent, national political issues have percolated down to the village level. 'Do you want *Ram-rajya* or *Ravana-rajya?*' runs one popular election slogan. As election day draws near, campaigns rush into a fever-pitch of rallies and door-to-door visits, rumours crisscross the summer air like fencing swords, and there is a last-minute effort to ban liquor on election day.

'A united village is much better,' sighs Syed Valiuddin Syed Moinuddin, one of the few Muslims in the village. Unity is an obvious preference for Moinuddin: he believes the Hindu-majority village will close ranks if the Muslims 'cross' any of them. 'Today there is a fight in every house.'

Ten years ago, this would never have happened in Metikheda, a small village that cockily straddles one of Yavatmal district's highways. The highway—with its cheeky teashop culture of slang—rules village life these days, a phenomenon that has old-timers up in arms. The highway is a landmark even otherwise: the bus-stop, hospital, and the school—which doubles up as election booth—are located here.

Since most of the 2,000 people living in Metikheda are tribal, the village was classified as an adivasi village in 1984. The main tribal groups include the Kunbis, Pardhans, Bhils, Gowaris, Gonds—and the Kolambs who worked as domestic labour for the Gonds when they ruled Gondwana. Each of these groups has its own separate *basti* or neighbourhood. Two other tribal groups, the Banjaras and the Bhois, live in Pilkhana, a congested basti across the river. The river, which is invisible from the main village, doubles up as the village brewery.

Although Metikheda lies in Yavatmal's cash-rich cotton belt, most residents don't benefit from it since they don't own land. A few landlords or *ijaradars* own all the land in Yavatmal district, which has the highest percentage of landless labour in Maharashtra. This landlessness, coupled with seasonal employment of eight months each year, manifests itself in poverty. More than 40 percent of Metikheda's families—150 out of 350 families—struggle below the poverty line. Several of the poorer families earn only Rs 240 a month.

Poverty—and its web of powerlessness—is as much part of Metikheda's landscape as the affluent Saroday family. The Sarodays are not just one more rich family; they are virtually Metikheda's Nehru-Gandhi dynasty. They own 125 acres of land, 25 high-yielding Jersey crossbred buffaloes, 10 handpumps, and employ 75 labourers—and were the first to introduce hybrid jowar in Metikheda. Their economic empire has now grown from cotton farming to include seed shops, shopping centres, mini-dairies, vegetable export businesses, and fertiliser agencies in Yavatmal district. Every day, two truckloads of vegetables leave Vijay Saroday's house for Andhra Pradesh.

Vijay Saroday, whose sons are educated in Nagpur and Pune, inherited this empire from his father, who is considered to be the village patriarch. His father contributed land during Vinoba Bhave's Bhoodan movement; even today 'the Saroday *kutumb* [family] brings *sukh shanti* [peace and happiness] to the village,' says Vijay, using the royal third person tense. Villagers perceive this somewhat differently; not only are there murmurs of corruption, but 'the Saroday family's whole attitude is that everyone is there to serve them,' says an old woman, Parvatibai Jaiswal.

Politically, the Sarodays have always been Metikheda's first family. A Saroday has been sarpanch for 27 out of 40 years. In the late eighties, the family controlled practically every political institution: while Vijay Saroday was a member of the Panchayat Samiti, his brother was the village policeman. Sarodays ran the village school and the sole flour mill. 'They didn't want to install electricity because they didn't want another flour mill to come to the village,' says Madhukar Mhatkar, who was independent sarpanch for four years. Today, although their political power has waned, they are still the largest employers in the village—with the absolute power to deny livelihoods to those who offend.

It is within this context that the 1989 victory of an all-women panel including disenfranchized Gond, dalit and Banjara women must be recognized for the landmark that it was. 'Only one family has ruled all these years,' says Maiah Wankhede, who became sarpanch of the women's panchayat. 'When such a family gets defeated by women . . . that means politically they are destroyed.'

The decision to put forward an all-women panchayat for the 1989 elections was an inevitable part of the social processes that the Wankhedes set into motion when they moved to Metikheda in 1980. Maiah, an activist of long standing, came from an urban middle-class background. Her grandfather, a *talati* (revenue officer) during the British Raj, had been given 960 acres of land in the Konkan. Maiah—then Kulkarni—grew up in Bombay, where she graduated in English Literature. Other family members still work as professionals in Bombay, or run businesses: Kulkarni Laboratories makes 'Chatpat', a tablet for headaches and fevers. 'I used to be such a spendthrift when I was young,' laughs Maiah. 'I used to buy so many clothes that no one believed I would be able to do political work. They predicted I'd be home in ten days.'

Maiah turned political during the Emergency, when she worked with Madhu Dandavate. During that time, she came in contact with Chandrakant Wankhede, an Amravati-born activist whom she later married. Chandrakant or Chandu, as he is popularly called, was then the state convenor of the Chhatra Yuva Sangharsh Vahini, a people's movement that aimed for a just distribution of development resources and land among the landless and poor peasantry. The Wankhedes' stint with the Vahini gave way to a lasting involvement with the Shetkari Sanghatana from 1985. Started by Sharad Joshi in Maharashtra in the early eighties, the Sanghatana is a peasant organization which locates rural poverty, underdevelopment and unemployment in the imbalance between an urban industrialized India and a rural agricultural Bharat.

Chandu and Maiah's decision to move to Metikheda grew out of both these influences: the Sanghatana's rural-based politics and the Vahini's work with landless labourers. Maiah, who has also done a B Ed degree, got a teaching job at Saroday's village school, and a room was rented from the local landlords. 'They were the only ones who had extra rooms,' says Chandu.

Meetings were held, and villagers—including women—started blocking the highway during Sanghatana protests demanding higher prices for farm produce. 'We would put almost 300 to 400 people on the highway.' But contradictions soon emerged. How could one organize landless labourers to demand minimum wages from their landlords, while staying in a landlord's house? Even as Maiah lost her job at the school, the Wankhedes bought four acres of wasteland on a *tekdi* or hilltop overlooking the village. By now, the tekdi has been transformed into an oasis of calm green, where the Wankhedes live with their dog Lilabai, grow organic vegetables and fruits for self-consumption—and Chandu indulges his passion for cultivating roses.

'Oh, my God,' worries Maiah on a particularly hot afternoon, when Lilabai has stopped eating chapatis in the heat and is being fed milk and the Glucose biscuits that we have brought with us. 'In the Sanghatana, we always used to look down on city people who fed their dogs milk and biscuits, while village people have nothing to eat. And here I am . . . 'City and village habits stand out strongly in this setting. 'When my friends used to come from Bombay and Poona, they required so much water . . . four-five mugs just to go to the toilet!' exclaims Maiah. 'My God, it is a luxury, we used to think, to spend so much water. I remember when I used to wash my clothes, in the last water I used to wash my utensils. But the government gives 40 litres of water per person for the villages, 80 litres per person in the cities, even though in villages we have animals to look after.'

In the 1989 elections, one of the symbols the women's panel used was that of a tiger. In Vijay Saroday's mind, the tiger is nothing but a symbol of danger. 'If he has a tiger sign, imagine what a dangerous man he is,' he says, referring to Chandu, who initiated the panel. For the village tribals, however, the tiger holds a more empowering connotation of strength. This anecdote is meant only to symbolize the wide gulf that stretches between the worldviews of Metikheda's landlords and the landless. But tiger or no tiger, most tribal men were sceptical of fielding an all-women panel. 'When we used to meet someone personally, they would agree,' remembers Maiah. 'But in group meetings, they would say 'How will they be able to work? What can they do?' Groups also feared that a women's panel would increase, rather than decrease, Saroday's chances of winning the election. It was finally agreed that an all-women panel should be elected *unopposed*.

This needed the cooperation of Saroday, who was himself planning to contest the election. 'So we went to his house and said, 'Let your wife and some other ladies be part of the panel. ' Only we told him his wife could not be sarpanch, because then the post of sarpanch would again go to the same house.' Saroday disagreed, mainly because he was confident of winning against a women's panel. Winning the 1989 gram panchayat elections meant much more than winning previous elections had. The government had just started the Jawahar Rozgar Yojana under which funds would be disbursed directly to villages. For the first time, gram panchayats would have control over a large pool of funds.

Despite Saroday's noncooperation, the Wankhedes decided to field a nine-women panel. One woman was chosen from each of the Gond, Bhil, Kolamb, dalit, Banjara, and other politically marginalized groups—while Maiah's name was proposed for sarpanch. 'I refused to be on it,' recalls Maiah. 'But then all of them got scared. And rumours spread that I am withdrawing because we are not confident of winning.' Once the panel was set up, the village women started campaigning for the first time. The women's panel slogan—*'paani, sandas, aani indhan'* (water, toilets and fuel)—came up everywhere. 'All the walls were covered the very first day,' says Maiah. 'Not a single wall was left for the opposition to write on.'

The opposition simply took the well-trodden political route of using culture, family pressure, money, liquor and political institutions to win elections. All these have gender-specific implications—in that they are all controlled by men—and very effective against women. Culture has always been a potent tool to keep women 'in their place'. This is mainly because each culture lays down strict norms which determine what roles men and women can play. Since most cultures define politics as a male role, any attempt by women to enter politics is viewed as a 'transgression', as 'going against the culture.' Cultural symbols are particularly effective weapons in keeping women in their place. The practice of wearing mangalsutras and putting *kumkum* are signs of marital status in Maharashtra. Maiah uses neither, an innocuous personal choice that became a loaded cultural weapon. 'They used to tell women, "if you vote for her, you won't be able to apply kumkum", says Maiah. 'Meaning you will become a widow. Your husband will die if you vote for her. It was very sensitive.'

Maiah's short hair—a symbol of widowhood in rural areas—was similarly turned against her, as was the fact that Maiah and Chandu don't have a child. '"Are you going to vote for that *vanjhoti* woman?" they would say,' says Maiah. '"Then you will also not have a child."' The Marathi word *'vanjhoti'* is particularly loaded—it means not just childless, but barren, unable to have children. In rural cultures where a woman's primary role is to reproduce, such weapons are potent reminders of the price of 'going against the culture'. 'When it is put that way, then the women do not dare,' says Maiah.

Since the family is the main institution through which culture reproduces itself, family pressure often prevents women from stepping outside culturally-ascribed female roles. In Metikheda too, the opposition sought to 'manufacture' such family pressure. A group of 10 men visited Chhabu, the Gond candidate with a letter from her 'husband' instructing her to withdraw from the elections. Chhabu, whose husband works outside the village, cannot read. 'I told them, "He may have written the letter, but I will contest the elections".'

Liquor can be seen as another gender-specific political tool. Free liquor is used primarily to induce men—liquor consumers—to vote for a particular party. But it has a wider, ripple effect on women who may not consume liquor. Men often swap their wives' votes for liquor. 'If you tell your wife to vote for us, we'll give you liquor,' explains Maiah. Rural women all over India—particularly during the Andhra Pradesh anti-arrack agitation—have testified how drunkenness is often accompanied by a web of violence which further subordinates women's independent decision-making capacities.

Money is another common weapon of India's political elites—the practice of buying votes is so common that it is often seen as 'natural'. Men—who constitute the 'political elite'—have access to monetary resources; women—who constitute the 'politically marginal'—do not. The women's panel claims that the opposition offered several economic inducements to impoverished tribals: a television set for community viewing, free bangles, snacks, blouse pieces, cash and foodgrains.

The all-women panel's counter-strategy against such tactics was unconventional—and effective. Maiah and Chandu requested liquor vendors to shut down for a few days. There are no government-licensed liquor shops in Metikheda; tribals brew liquor near the river out of mahua and other forest produce. Since brewing liquor is also a source of livelihood, curtailing it hurts the economic interests of tribal families, who are also voters. In a compromise, vendors agreed to shut shop for the crucial 72 hours leading up to the election.

On 7 June, a day when a tribal festival called Mrig takes place, the panel held a village meeting. Metikheda's tribals had not celebrated Mrig for several years because of a sheer absence of means. 'Here is the opportunity,' Maiah told them at the meeting. 'Enjoy it. Take the money and presents. It is not a bribe—it is your right. For years, they have squeezed you. How has this one person become rich while you have stayed poor?' Maiah also asked them to analyse why they were being given money—now. 'The next day, he stopped giving money. He realized that people will take what he gives and probably not vote for him.'

Another equally effective strategy was used the night before the elections—when the opposition was expected to make a last-ditch attempt at buying votes. The panel decided it would stay awake all night along with its supporters. 'We will play, we will sing, whatever, but we will not sleep.' A bunch of male Sanghatana activists set up an all-night observation post on the lane outside Saroday's house. 'That is the only lane through which they can come out,' laughs Maiah. 'Till 4:30 am, they were stuck inside the house.' The adivasi women danced through the night. 'At five o'clock, in the daylight, they didn't have the courage to come out and distribute money.'

Since Saroday's brother was then police patil—giving Saroday access to this political institution—the women's panel decided not to rely on any police assistance during the elections. So when they discovered five bogus voters on election day, they just waited for other government officials to arrive. 'They were nomads who had just been picked up and brought to the booth,' says Maiah. 'They were outsiders voting against the names of villagers.' Bogus voters are easily identified in a village, where everyone knows everyone else. After a major shindig involving the police, presiding officers and senior government officials, the women's panel decided not to press charges. 'It is our experience,' says Maiah, 'that the real culprits will escape and these poor people will go to jail.'

Election day was a milestone in Metikheda's history. For the first time, an all-women panel was elected to the gram panchayat. For the first time, close to 100 percent of the women in the village turned out to cast their vote, a factor which contributed to the panel's victory. Women trudged miles, rode in on bullock carts, while old women were carried in on relatives' backs. 'A spirit was created,' recalls Maiah. The same evening, when the results were announced, a wave of jubilation hit the village. The women went on a three-hour victory procession around the village, which was decorated with rangoli. When the rally passed Vidyabai Jaiswal's house, Vidyabai—the co-opted female member on earlier panchayats—came out and washed the feet of all the elected women. Washing another's feet is a ceremonial honour typically reserved for men, for example when a bridegroom enters his in-laws' house after marriage. 'A zamindar [landlord] lady, she herself washed the feet of dalit and adivasi women,' says Maiah.

'It was something really great. We found it so touching at that time.'

Other than Maiah, the elected women included Rampyari Jaiswal, a landed widow; Chhabu Ghodam, a Gond orphan who had grown up under Rampyari's wing; Usha Dawde, who lived across the highway; Kalawati Waghade, from the Kolamb caste, Dharmi Aade from the Banjara community; and two neighbours, Kamla Khadse and Annapurna Thackeray, whose families owned 50 acres each of land. The ninth member, Pramila Jawade, seems the most individualistic. A dalit neo-Buddhist, she came here from another village with her lover who was already married. Their three pretty daughters learn dancing; their father—Pramila's lover or husband, no one is sure—takes them by turn once a week to Yavatmal for a treat. It is seriously depressing to hear that Pramila, who looks and talks like a well-built sturdy and strong-minded woman is beaten up by this man every other day.

From the start, the panchayat worked to ensure that all its programmes met the ends of distributive justice. The previous panchayat had selectively implemented government schemes, mainly in elite areas. For the first time, services also reached marginal dalit and tribal communities. It is instances like these that bear out activist Gail Omvedt's conclusion that 'when women come into local political power as part of a collective fight, they do so with a bias towards the low castes and peasants among them.'

Fuel and water were the first two schemes to be implemented. 'My first step, our very first step, was to get 100 percent smokeless *chulhas* [stoves],' says Maiah. The beneficial impact of smokefree stoves on women's health is already well documented. Although the panchayat distributed subsidized stoves to a number of households in Metikheda, the smokeless chulha scheme failed to take off. Maiah attributes the scheme's failure to a basic defect in design. One, the stoves were too small for the women to cook the large round jowar bhakris that are the family staple. Two, a chimney-like pipe designed to funnel smoke out of the house, actually accomplished the opposite: it allowed rainwater in during the monsoons.

'In my pipe, because of the water collecting, there used to be frogs constantly,' says Maiah. 'They used to shit in that and an awful smell used to come.' Maiah still kept her stove 'because so many government people used to come and see our smokeless chulha experiment. I thought it should at least be there in the sarpanch's house. Of course, I never used to cook on that.'

Along with smokeless chulhas, the panchayat also initiated a gobar gas scheme. The first 40 gobar gas plants were sanctioned in the panchayat's first year. Maiah points out that the panchayat never discriminated between supporters and opposition in the allocation of all schemes. 'Whatever forms would come, we would just arrange them according to the date of receipt, and give connections in that order.'

In rural areas, the politics of water is inextricably linked with the politics of power. This was much the case in Metikheda in 1989. Although a tapwater scheme had been sanctioned during the previous panchayat's tenure, the tapwater was being diverted into the fields of two large farmers. Private house taps had only been given to a few elite families; the bulk of the village clustered around eight community taps where water was available for one hour every day. 'There used to be fights every day at the community taps,' remembers Maiah. 'The women used to come and complain that someone else was not allowing them to take water.' As a result, villagers started cutting water pipes in a fit of pique: 'if I can't get it, you also won't get it.'

In such situations, any attempt to widen access to water constitutes a major challenge to existing power structures. Nevertheless, the women's panchayat took this on, studying and mapping the village's underground water resources as a first step. The following steps were then taken to make water freely available to all.

i. A valve was placed to block the diversion of community water to the two wealthy farmers. This one step immediately made more water available for community use.
ii. Several community taps were constructed. Today, the number of community taps has increased from 12 to 20. Many of these are in dalit and tribal areas. As a result, there are fewer fights at community taps.
iii. Private tap connections were sanctioned to anybody who could afford an initial deposit of Rs 400 and water tax of Rs 15.

The number of private house taps has shot up from 10 under the previous panchayat to 110 today. This benefits almost 300 houses, according to Maiah, since there is less pressure on community taps—and because immediate neighbours fill water at these house taps. 'In villages, no one says no to sharing water.'

As a result of these measures, the quantum of water provided each day has increased threefold: from 40,000 cubic litres to 120,000 cubic litres and from 1 hour to 3 hours each day. The Panchayat Samiti has also sanctioned a supplementary tank for Metikheda. While increasing the supply of water, the panchayat ensured that water resources were not overexploited. On one line, where many private taps had been sanctioned, water pressure started diminishing at houses at the end of the line. The panchayat immediately stopped giving new connections on that line. Although this step has angered individual applicants, it does serve community interests.

Before the women's first year in office had ended, they had also taken up other schemes. About 16 new electric poles have been constructed, mainly in poorer areas. Everyone has not got electricity, but there is an electric pole within 100 feet of their house. According to government rules, this means they will not have to pay for the pole when applying for house electricity—only the cost of the electric metre. Even so, most of Metikheda's tribal families still cannot afford house electrification.

Toilets were identified by the panchayat as another priority area, particularly since Metikheda is on a highway. 'It really is a problem for women to find place to go to the toilet,' explains Maiah. 'They have to go to faraway fields.' But no women use the community toilet built by the panchayat. It is difficult to fathom why. One woman says the toilets are dirty and badly-maintained. Another says they are unaccustomed to such toilets. Unlike the community toilet, which seems to be a universal disaster, other constructions have not turned into white elephants. A primary school is in use, sewage channels have been dug, dhobi ghats or washing platforms built near community taps provide a clean washing area for women. Kuccha roads have been paved into all-weather roads, and a community wedding hall has been built in the dalit basti.

After it had shown tangible results in its first year, the panchayat launched its second year with a programme that proved decidedly unpopular: collecting taxes. The previous panchayat had collected about Rs 6,000 in house, water, and electricity taxes only from 193 houses it had numbered. Almost 150 unnumbered houses fell outside the tax net. After systematically numbering all the houses, the women's panchayat demanded they pay their taxes. 'There was a big disturbance,' remembers Maiah. 'They said, 'So far, no one has asked us for tax. Why are you asking us?'' To increase tax collection, the panchayat decided to stop allocating domicile certificates to families that had not paid their taxes. These proof-of-residence certificates are essential to avail of bank loans under government schemes like IRDP. 'If you want the certificate, pay your taxes,' the panchayat told them.

Although this novel linkage ensured that tax collection shot up from Rs 6,000 to almost Rs 20,000 per year, it also made the panchayat unpopular among the poorer groups who were its prime constituency—but who now experienced the tax burden most heavily. And although tax collection now stands at a whopping 97 percent—and the panchayat has a healthy bank balance of Rs 53,000—the controversial 'tax for certificates' plan emerged as a major issue in Metikheda's 1995 panchayat election.

The decision to collect taxes has indirectly benefited the village: it has given the panchayat an independent financial base which it can use for maintenance expenses. 'Now we can repair taps, bulbs and so on ourselves,' explains Maiah. 'The previous panchayat could not save anything, so they could not spend anything.' This emphasis on maintenance and repair is a central feature of the women's panchayat. 'We repair anything within 24 hours,' explains Maiah. 'This is the only gram panchayat with this philosophy. We don't wait for the zilla parishad. It takes at least 15 days for them to repair anything.' This policy too comes out of a deep understanding of women's issues. 'For 15 days, there is no water,' says Maiah. 'And we had mainly decided that women should not have any water problem. So even if there is a pump failure, within 24 hours we manage it.'

If raising tax collection and funding repairs are issues that most panchayats rarely concern themselves with, fighting corruption is an issue that gram panchayats never touch. But corruption is so much a part and parcel of Panchayati Raj that Rajiv Gandhi once estimated that only 15 percent of the amount sanctioned for rural development actually reached beneficiaries. Opportunities for corruption abound at all levels. In the gram panchayat, the sarpanch and the gram sevak have greatest access to corruption, since they pass estimates, receive funds, distribute payments and jointly sign cheques.

One of the Shetkari Sanghatana's main objectives in capturing political power was to combat rural corruption—and free up development funds. In keeping with this, the women's panchayat dismissed two gram sevaks who were suspected of financially manipulating village funds. Both gram sevaks have since been suspended by the zilla parishad which employs them. The women's panchayat has combated corruption in another less formalized way: simply by checking the prices of goods, challenging inflated bills, and ensuring that all bought materials are consumed—not wasted, pilfered or diverted for personal profit. During the community toilet construction, the Panchayat Samiti engineer estimated that each toilet seat would cost Rs 475; the women bought exactly the same toilet seats for Rs 90 a piece. 'They had bought that same third-rate coverless seat of cheapest quality and put the bill for Rs 475.'

But the fight against corruption has had a mixed impact on the village. On the one hand, people readily acknowledge that lower corruption has brought with it development benefits. 'Earlier panchayats had spent a lot of money, but no work had been seen,' says Ankush Khadse. On the other hand, government officials are hesitant to work in Metikheda—where there is low opportunity for corruption. Thus fewer development schemes are sanctioned for the village. 'So the opposition started saying, look these people are doing nothing,' says Maiah. 'In other gram panchayats, so much work is being done.' This may have stalled the sanction of a private latrine scheme. 'Many people wanted a private latrine and there is a government scheme for that. But for one reason or another, they are not giving it. The actual reason, I know, is if I don't look at how they build it, they will come tomorrow and do it. But they know we will be standing there, seeing how much cement they use.'

> 'I've spent 60 years in this village. Nothing had been done before the women came to power. Nothing.'
>
> —Parvati Ramnath Jaiswal

> 'The amount of work that the ladies did, the men will not do.' —Syed Valiuddin Syed Moinuddin

'For 40 years, nobody had paid attention to the issue of water. But nine women were elected, and the water problem became much less.' — Marutrao Gangaram Atram

Yes, there are also rumbles of discontent. *Garibala kai nahi* [nothing for the poor],' says Panchphula Nikhade, who wants a tap near her house. Syed Moinuddin says there is no doctor at the primary health centre. 'This is the work of the gram panchayat.' A Kolamb tribal grumbles that the road to their colony crumbles every monsoon, and Vijay Saroday says Metikheda has been pushed back by 10 years. But, by and large, all Metikheda—men and women, landed and landless—is united in the belief that the women's panchayat has done what a traditional, male panchayat had not. Its work has created ripples outside—the next village of Mohda is using Metikheda's water supply scheme as a model; another village, Khora, in the same district put up an all-women panel in the 1995 elections. 'When we go out and tell people we're from Metikheda, we feel proud,' says Parvati Jaiswal.

The panchayat—simply by taking up issues other panchayats ignore—has also had a ripple effect within the village. Sunita Patil tells how a group of women have been given a Rs 15,000 loan to buy and rear goats under the government's Development of Women and Children in Rural Areas scheme. Although the scheme had existed for seven years, she says, leaning on the gate, 'we didn't know about it till Maiah got us the information.' In Pilkhana, the Banjara-Bhoi settlement of 35 families, a group of men and women explain that the panchayat is trying to build a *gaothan* (community grazing land) on a plot appropriated by an affluent farmer. 'In the land records, that plot was a gaothan,' says an indignant man. 'But no one before Maiah had tried to do anything.'

If villagers keep referring to Maiah, rather than the women's panchayat, it is merely an acknowledgement of Maiah's central role in that panchayat. Although each panchayat member is allocated a portfolio—such as health, adult literacy, water, electricity—it is universally recognized that Maiah drives the panchayat. But while there is no doubt that this has contributed to Metikheda's rapid development, it has also resulted in an excessively centralized panchayat. Even though Maiah may be a model sarpanch—who has broadened the definition of a gram panchayat—such centralization may not help to empower all the women members.

Other contradictions have surfaced during this experience. On the one hand, women have entered the political arena in a very real sense—by fighting elections; not through political patronage or through patriarchal largesse. But this process of mobilization has had a dual effect: it has simultaneously united and divided village women. On the one hand, a women's panchayat has given women—regardless of caste and class—a chance to identify, unite around, and articulate common needs and problems: water, fuel, fodder and alcoholism. On the other hand, a women's panchayat has also given political interests a chance to divide women—using caste, class and money—into political factions. 'Women won't unite because it's a two-party village,' explains Chandrabhau Patil. 'They will go with their parties.'

Rampyari Jaiswal, the deputy sarpanch on the women's panchayat, is a case in point. In the 1995 elections, Rampyari has decided to vote for the opposition. 'I am not with Maiahtai any more,' she says, grinning toothily. 'I made demands which weren't met.' Rampyari, who can sign her name in English, says she asked Maiah for buffaloes to use on her land. Maiah refused. Since Saroday has promised her a tractor, she'll vote for him instead.

Another contradiction that is evident in the Metikheda panchayat is its complete success in addressing certain basic women's issues—such as water and fodder—and its complete inability to address other, more complex women's issues—such as alcoholism. The contrast is shown in the next page.

Why could women agitate for fodder but not against liquor? Perhaps because men were ready to support an agitation around fodder, which does not confront male interests, but were reluctant to support an agitation against liquor, which directly confronts such interests. Several feminist writers have alluded to the difficulties that women face when raising such issues. Madhu Kishwar writes how an NGO in Andhra Pradesh was unable to recruit women carpenters even though it was a paid job—the men would not allow women to take up this job. 'The activist found that her work with women was acceptable to the men only as long as they could see the immediate benefits to the family without challenging the power of men.' Similarly, agitating for fodder benefits the family; agitating against liquor is not seen to do so.[1]

Writers like Carolyn Moser use the terms 'practical gender needs' and 'strategic gender interests' to distinguish between women's issues like fodder and alcoholism. Practical gender needs are those that derive from the traditional division of labour—looking after children, filling water, cooking for the family etc. Women's attempts to meet these needs—by securing access to water, land, housing, fuel and so on—benefit the fa ly without confronting male interests.[2] Strategic gender neea: on the other hand, arise from women's attempts to confront this traditional package: gender roles, division of labour, male dominance and privilege. Women's attempts to meet these needs—by fighting against rape, unequal wages, alcoholism, domestic violence—usually confront male interests and are resisted. Typically, it is much easier to meet women's practical needs than to address women's strategic interests.

FODDER

In 1992, when there was a major drought in the area, almost 1,200 cattle had died in Metikheda and its surrounding villages. There was no fodder in the village, but the Forest Department did not allow cattle to graze in the forest. One day, the villagers—led by the women—collected about 850 animals, and let them loose in the jungle. 'We told the guard to do whatever he wants. We will not allow our animals to die because there is no fodder in the village. It is our right to use this forest because it is the right of the animals to survive.'

Local folklore has it that the guard asked his boss for advice. The boss told his guard not to take action. 'Because if this is published in the paper, all the other villages will do the same thing.' In this way, women solved a temporary fodder crisis.

LIQUOR

'Our village is number one in drinking and gambling,' says a Gond woman. Women say that alcoholism is a major problem: 90 percent of men drink and beat up their wives. A group of women themselves approached Maiah to take up this issue.

The women took out a signature campaign, wrote a letter to the district police, and called a street-corner meeting with the men. But at the meeting, not one woman dared speak, fearing retribution from their husbands.

'You think you're too smart, you're the only one who opened her mouth.' A few rallies and so on were planned, but never happened. 'Many women come up to me and say they expected me to do something about alcoholism,' says Maiah. 'But I couldn't succeed.'

Women are nowhere on the agenda as the May 1995 gram panchayat elections unfold. Maiah—dubbed sarpanch *mahoday* (imprecisely, Her Highness)—by rivals, is not contesting. 'We always accuse people of clinging to the chair. Then how can I contest again?' Both the Gaos and the Raos have the requisite 30 percent women on their panels. 'I have given birth to three sons and one daughter, but I have never walked around the village,' says the Rao panel's Annapurna Chincholkar.

All Metikheda avidly discusses how a woman—Kunda Saroday—was publicly insulted by Chandu Wankhede. Chandu, whom the opposition had apparently likened to Ravana, retorted at a public meeting thus: 'If I am Ravana, I should carry away Sita [meaning Saroday's wife].' Although Chandu insists he was jesting, several women—including Maiah—feel uneasy about the comment. 'How do you think my son felt on hearing this about his mother?' asks Saroday, quick to seize political capital. 'A few murders would have happened.' Both sides are quick to make political capital out of nothing, even our visit. Saroday says the Gao panel campaign is billing us as fat cats from Mumbai who will bring gains to the village. No village campaign is big enough for journalistic objectivity—or family ties. Khadse's nephew, who helped his daughter elope with an outsider, has crossed over to the other side. Another Khadse, Babytai, who is on the Panchayat Samiti, has refused to endorse any of the panels.

Rumours buzz like hungry flies—arms and ammunitions have entered the village, buzz, buzz, buzz. Chandu and Ankush frantically count expected votes late into the night. A fracas is avoided at the election booth as someone bruises a rival candidate; Maiah and the women rush over to a Gond house where liquor is clandestinely being sold; in the midst of the *hungama* an old woman announces that she will vote for the panel that gives her a saree. 'Everyone will come in good clothes. How can I go vote in this raggedy saree?'

It is with infinite regret that I later digest the news that the Gao panel lost all its seats to the Rao panel in the May 1995 elections.

NOTES

1. Madhu Kishwar, Nature of Women's Mobilisation in Rural India, *Economic and Political Weekly* (24-31 Dec 1988)
2. Carolyn Moser, Gender Planning in the Third World : Meeting Practical and Strategic Gender Needs, *World Development* 17, 11 (1989)

VITNER

Sonali Sathaye

'People say the men of Vitner are like women.'

Anjubai's son is getting married. There is to be a party exclusively for the women tonight. The ground outside her house has been swept clean and spread with *dhurries,* leaving a little open space for the dancers. Susheelabai is clearly a favourite among the women gathered here. The dance, interspersed with snatches of dialogue which falls back into a high-pitched chorus, is uninhibited, often derisive of husbands and their ilk, often openly sexual in nature. Tea is served at 11 at night to the tired, excited women, their faces flushed with the pleasure and energy of complicity. The evening has been loud, exuberant, festive.

The next day, we walk over a stubbly hill in the burning heat of a three o'clock sun. Looking down for the stones as we descend the short hill, I suddenly notice that the women do not wear chappals—the husbands have on pairs of white plastic shoes. 'Why do you not wear chappals?'

'We are women.'

'And so?'

'Amongst us we are not allowed to wear footwear in the presence of our husbands and village elders.'

When they enter the village from a visit to Jalgaon or Chopda, women take off their chappals and hold them in their hand, entering the village appropriately, in bare feet, regardless of the season or time of day.

Vitner is a tiny village on the banks of the Tapi in the hinterland of Maharashtra, surrounded on all sides by fields of sugarcane and cotton. It is connected to the nearest town, the Jalgaon district headquarters at Chopda, by State Transport. The buses which come right up to the village square, were initiated by the women's panchayat. Until then, the buses would stop at Tonda, a village 5 km from Vitner. The journey from Chopda to Vitner is itself a two-hour ride across a bone-rattling, pothole-ridden track which must be a torture in the monsoon.

The village is dominated by the Gujjars and the Kolis, both farming communities. The single largest population of Gujjars in Maharashtra is reportedly in Jalgaon district, where the most common Gujjar surname is Patil. They are a flamboyant people, whose dress, language and customs show distinct links with the people of Rajasthan and Gujarat. The women are tall and big-boned, brightly bejewelled. The men too are striking, often with light eyes and fair skins. Festive occasions are celebrated with much loud, exuberant singing and dancing, especially among the women.

The Kolis (no relation to the fisherfolk of coastal Maharashtra) are much more subdued, even timid. Raisingh is a typical Koli name, although some adivasis may also share the name. In general the Kolis are poorer than the Gujjars, although in Vitner neither community is conspicuously better off. Kolis and Gujjars speak Ahirani, a lilting mixture of Marathi, Gujarati and Hindi—a dialect which they view as inferior to standard Marathi, and so are embarrassed to talk on first acquaintance. Although the Kolis are considered to be of a lower caste than the Gujjars, there is little evidence of division along caste lines, apart from the usual grouping of houses in bastis according to caste.

But apart from the two traditional communities, Vitner has a third, important community to whom many of its people bear as strong—if not stronger—allegiance. The Shetkari Sanghatana's ideas and philosophy are the invisible third in the phenomenon that is Vitner. Ghanshyam Patil, a Gujjar farmer, has devoted all his time and energy to promoting the cause of the Sanghatana. He openly declares that Sanghatana leader Sharad Joshi is his guru, calling him a *marg-darshak* (guide), a *mahan atma*, a *daivat* (a godly being). On his right fist, Ghanshyam wears a large blue-green Sanghatana tattoo. One entire room of his two-room house has been decorated with pictures of Joshi, newspaper clippings of his speeches and rallies, and quotes from his speeches. These have been made into charts and mounted onto what space remains.

Ghanshyam's daughter Sulochana was married in March 1995 at the age of fourteen, along with her sister Indira, ten. Both will stay with their family until they have finished the Class X exams. Sulochana's father-in-law has promised to educate her till Class XII and let her work in a lawyer's office thereafter. Sulochana is not happy at this: she had hoped to become a lawyer herself. Sulochana's father and extended family—all dedicated Sanghatana workers—know how she feels about this marriage. 'Why not let her wait for a while?' 'In our *samaj*,' says one of them, 'girls get married early, especially if there is a good offer. If a girl waits until she is 17 or 18, people start to wonder what is wrong with her. What can we do, that is the way our samaj functions.' 'What if Sharad Joshi were to ask you to wait until your daughters were 18 before you married them?' I ask. The talk of *'aamcha samaj'* (our community) abruptly ceases. 'Then we'd do it.' 'Even if it meant going against your community?' 'Even if it meant that,' Ghanshyam responds with fierce loyalty.

In November 1986, four tractors full of people from Vitner, men and women, travelled to the historic Chandwad conference in Nasik district, where the issue of women's participation in politics was formalized. In April the next year, the gram sabha decided to elect an all-women panchayat in Vitner village. As at all gram sabhas, only the men of the village were present. In this Sanghatana stronghold, women who were approached to be members of the council were wives of Sanghatana sympathizers and workers who had travelled to Nagpur, Parbhani, Nanded, and Delhi to attend Sanghatana gatherings. A nine-women panel stood for elections: Shubhatai Raisingh, Indirabai Patil, Susheelabai Patil, Rukmabai Patil, Radhabai Patil, Sakwarbai Raisingh, Kamalbai Raisingh, Shantabai Raisingh, and Dwarkabai Raisingh. Of these, one (Dwarkabai) was adivasi, the rest were evenly divided between Kolis and Gujjars.With the sole exception of Indirabai, who was later to become deputy sarpanch, all the rest of the women were at first reluctant and hesitant to take on the challenge. 'We were completely uneducated and so we didn't think we could do it,' says one of them.

The nine members contested from three wards. They canvassed in a group in the evenings and nights, going from house to house, promising to 'end all disputes', to 'carry the village forward', according to Shubhatai Raisingh. Indirabai says they did not promise anything, they asked for a 'chance', just once, pointing out that the men who had been in charge all these years had not done much for the village. A Shiv Sena-backed panel constituted the opposition (although not officially recognized as such, as party elections are disallowed at the gram panchayat level). Of their eight members—one member contested from two wards—two were women. In the election that followed, the women emerged victorious. Indirabai says they had vowed not to celebrate their victory, if even a single one of them had lost. To prevent it from seeming like the Gujjars had monopolized power, a half-reluctant Shubhatai Raisingh—a Koli—was made the sarpanch. Indirabai, a flamboyant Gujjar, was made the deputy sarpanch.

The personalities of the two women who would lead the panchayat at Vitner for the next five years are radically different. Shubhatai Raisingh is a small, timid-looking Koli woman in her late forties or early fifties. She lives with her husband, son, daughter-in-law and two grandsons in a thatched mud house that points to a somewhat precarious monetary condition. In the beginning, she prefers to stay in the background, letting her vociferous husband do the talking, apparently embarrassed to speak Ahirani. While I am urging her to speak, the crowd that has gathered around the newcomer tells how she used to be extremely frightened of new people, how the minute she saw the police she would hide.

The first time I meet Indirabai Patil, she is sitting in the centre of an admiring circle. It is early February. The throng comprises well-wishers and campaigners who would like to see Indirabai in the Vidhan Sabha this year. Her opponent is Arun Gujarathi, a Congress(I) candidate and cabinet minister in Sharad Pawar's government in Bombay. The Patils live in a small but well-equipped house—complete with television, telephone, and mixer—in the new housing complex in fast-developing Chopda, the taluka headquarters. Indirabai is a self-assured, fluent speaker who rarely pauses between sentences. She seems to carry with her the small assembly, stabbing the air with her fingers, raising one finger in the air, raising her voice over the constant din of the supporters when she wants to make a particular point. She is clearly in power. Her husband appears later, but the arrival does not cause much change in the arrangement—he is only introduced as Indirabai's husband, before she starts to speak again. Where Shubhatai is small and self-effacing, Indirabai fills the room with her presence. The lady sitting opposite me, in her sleeveless blouse, short hair and shaped eyebrows is not likely to go unnoticed in any place. Although officially deputy sarpanch, Indirabai

Bhanudas Patil has been described as 'kingmaker' among other things—a title she is not ashamed of.

Shubhatai tells a delightful story about an early exploit of their panchayat. About 52 acres of common land was being overrun by trespassers from outside the village. The nine women devised a simple solution, something the previous panchayat had been unable to do. They set the cattle loose in the field. The land is now being cultivated as an orchard, under the government's *vanikaran* (forestry) scheme—so that it brings in money which forms part of the panchayat fund.

Over the next five years, the new panchayat effected several changes in the village. It built seven rooms in the adivasi basti, added two schoolrooms to the already existing structure, one school compound, and several smooth cement inclines on the way to nearby Vadoda and Wadki, where the children go to school. Two new rooms were also built in the main village square during this period, one of which is used as the gram panchayat office, the other as an anganwadi or nursery for children.

Before the women came into power, the village school taught only until Class IV. Students were expected to go to Wadki and eventually Vadoda, if they wanted to study further. Now the village school has officially been extended up to Class VIII. But due to a lack of sufficient teachers, it actually functions only up to Class VII. Nonetheless, this has meant that students—especially girls whose education was discontinued after Class IV—can now study up to Class VII.

In 1989, its very first year of functioning, the panchayat made a *magni* (demand) to the local Member of Parliament for 29 electricity poles to add to the existing 30. Eight poles had arrived by February 1995, and the other 20 were expected shortly. The following year, in response to another magni made by the women—Shubhatai and Indirabai met the local MP Arun Gujarathi in Chopda—Vitner was granted a huge water tank which now dominates the village square. He also funded a pipeline which runs through the entire village. At present Vitner has 10 water connections, with 20 taps, one in every basti. The bus service was also extended upto Vitner during this period, at the instance of the panchayat. The bus halted at Tonda earlier, from where it was a long walk to the village. The panchayat has also built toilets for men and women in the square. Susheelabai, a member of the panchayat, even presumed to remember that they cost Rs 3,000. The toilets are not used, however, except by the men. The women do not like these; they find these 'dirty' and uncomfortable. Also, women who do not use the fields as their toilet hardly ever step out of the house. They find it odd to walk all the way across the village to the toilet—when they can just duck behind their houses instead.

Shubhatai remembers that the very first project their panchayat tackled was that of *darubandi* or prohibition. The reason offered for taking it is that *'Sharad Joshinni bayanna sangitle hote'*—Sharad Joshi had asked the women to. As in other villages where total prohibition is claimed to exist, the only difference is that shops selling it no longer openly exist. Those who wish to drink have to seek the brew in the adivasi basti instead.

Dwarkabai Raisingh, the sole adivasi member of the panchayat is too busy cleaning and preparing to move into her new concrete house to really talk with me. She is a tall wiry woman who looks like she will not take any nonsense from anyone. I have barely opened my mouth to tell her why I am there, when she tells me that she knows exactly what I want and will meet me later. I hover about the basti nevertheless and finally begin talking to a young man who does not appear to be doing much. He is educated, a Class XII pass from Amberner, a nearby village where most of the young men of the village go on to study. For some reason they all choose to study geography. He tells me that the Harijan basti used to be on top of the hill, where the water tank has now been built, but they had to abandon the area as the population rose and there was not enough water any more. They themselves had lived in the basti for seven or eight years without water. He says that the present panchayat has done nothing much for the basti, other than build a platform (*pharshi*) recently. I ask about the tap standing at the entrance to the basti. He concedes that it is thanks to this panchayat that they have water. But, he says, the Mangkolis who live only a few huts away do not have any water.

I finally meet Dwarkabai. She is still in a tearing hurry but agrees to take some time off. She is evidently disgruntled with the panchayat, although she will not tell me why outright. All I can gather is that the panchayat has not done enough for the adivasis, although there are few concrete charges. Later I hear from others, including Indirabai and Radhubai, that Dwarkabai hoped to get one of the seven rooms allotted to the adivasis and was displeased to find that her name was not given priority over the others in her community.

When I ask her if she attends meetings regularly, she guffaws loudly. 'Attend meetings? Who has the time to attend meetings at ten o'clock in the morning?' This too—like the problem with the smokeless chulhas and the toilets—is a complaint that is as frequently heard in Vitner, as, for example, in other villages where women are on the panchayat. Not many women can afford to drop work in the fields—which are often an hour's walk from the village—to attend such morning meetings. When there is a meeting however, who talks the most? Susheelabai says everybody does. Sakwarbai says Indirabai does. And Shubhatai says she does.

Shubhatai is not embarrassed to refer to the panchayat as 'her' panel, 'her' ward, 'her' idea. As such, she is able to quote some figures—that one schoolroom built in 1994 cost Rs 40,000, the money came out of the Jawahar Rozgar Yojana. But she constantly turns to her husband for confirmation on matters of finance. Interestingly, Dashrath Koli Raisingh, her husband, seems able to oblige her with facts and figures at all times—including the little detail that the cement for the incline toward Wadki came from the Block Development Officer.

The other panchayat members—barring Indirabai who regularly looked after the panchayat finances till she moved to Chopda—are unable to help with such information. Susheelabai Patil tells me the school compound built in 1989 cost Rs 8,000; sarpanchbai tells me the same compound cost Rs 10,000, while her nephew, the gram sipahi and I check the records to find that in fact Rs 21,000 was spent on the project. Members are also confused about schemes that the panchayat administers. What Susheelabai calls 'zilla parishad money' is in fact discovered to be 'JRY money' (although this could be an informal way of defining it, since most panchayat funds do emanate from the zilla parishad). And Shubhatai has not heard of the Integrated Rural Development Programme, set up for people below the poverty line, and whose execution she, as sarpanch, is supposed to oversee. Every now and again—when asked about the nitty-gritty of financial transactions—Shubhatai says she does not know, that she cannot read or write and has had to rely on the gram sevak and sipahi for information. *'Mi tar angtha, mala kay samajnar?'* (I am illiterate, what am I to understand?)

Her inability to read and write had caused her much pain in her dealings with the first gram sevak, a Mr Kale, whom both husband and wife say has cheated the panchayat out of a lot of money. They say he took advantage of Shubhatai's illiteracy—and got her to sign a paper authorizing him to operate the joint account at Wadki on his own. (Typically, both the sarpanch and gram sevak jointly operate the panchayat account.) The real story of what happened appears impossible to unravel. Even while Shubhatai and Dashrath Raisingh agitatedly froth at the mention of his name, Indirabai and Bhanudas Patil swear by his honesty.

Whatever the truth, the incident points to the state of utter dependency, upon husbands and gram sevaks, forced upon women—whether they be panchayat members or sarpanches—by a lack of basic literacy. This sense of dependence breeds an insecurity that works to undermine their own sense of worth and sense of power.

Is there a difference between an all-women panchayat and an all-male panchayat? If there is one, what is it and why? The response to these questions was uniformly the same. 'Men are more dishonest,' 'Men waste money on alcohol and pleasure,' 'Women do not fight—fight less—among themselves,' 'More work gets done by the women.' The responses did not vary according to gender: apparently both men and women consider an all-women panchayat more efficient and less corrupt than the traditional male one.

Could a male panchayat have done what this panchayat has achieved, in terms of bringing facilities to the villages? The response to this question varies between men and women. The women say that it could not, that they have been in power for so many years without the village seeing much improvement. The men—the gram sevak and the sarpanch who was in term just before Shubhatai, a Rambhau Patil, in particular—point out that earlier panchayats were not able to do as much, because the panchayats did not receive as much money then as they do now. This is a point to be noted, as it is true that the Jawahar Rozgar Yojana—the main regular source of panchayat funding—was only launched in 1989.

Despite all the praise for the women, when asked whether the village will re-elect an all-women panchayat, there seems to be a consensus that it will not. The gram sevak, Mr Bawa, has told the women that there cannot be another women's panchayat—Chief Election Commissioner T. N. Seshan has himself decreed it. Even though we would like to elect an all-women panchayat, we cannot, our hands are tied by the government, is the constant refrain heard through the viilage, any time this question comes up. Mr. Bawa backs away hastily when directly asked if he has the government circular that states that only two women may be included in the panchayat this year. Although it is not in writing, he lets it be known that this is what is implied by the government. There is a ready suspension of disbelief once the spectre of a *sarkari dhoran* (government policy) is raised—and if it were needed, the invocation of Mr. Seshan's name in this context is enough reason for the decision to be accepted without a murmur.

Men and women point out that it really does not matter whether or not an all-women panchayat comes to power again. The women of Vitner have all the *hakka* (rights) anyway, says one Gujjar woman, the hakka to own property being the most prominent among these. Her statement highlights a visible confidence found in a sizeable number of women in Vitner—especially Gujjar women and even women who are not panchayat members. Perhaps it is this confidence that makes many of the women eager to be part of village decision-making—a feeling singularly absent among women who are not panchayat members in other villages with all-women panchayats.

Some of the self-assurance stems from a sense of independence, which in itself, is born of a sense of financial security. To the women of Vitner, the panchayat is not the only forum available to assert themselves. In a village of 271 families, women from nearly 127 families are already the owners of land ranging between one to six acres. Indirabai says there are at least 60 applications waiting to be processed.

The second 'radical' resolution adopted at Chandwad in November 1986 concerned land rights for women. In the words of activist Gail Omvedt, the resolution 'went beyond the empty slogan of a "common civil code" to outline the means whereby women might claim a share in their parent's movable and immovable property and in the joint property of their family of marriage in the event of divorce or separation.[1] Even poor peasant women (who came) forward to speak on this expressed their claim. 'We want our share [*hissa*].'

The resulting Lakshmi Mukti programme was inaugurated during the Hingoli conference of November 1989—named after the village near Amraoti where the conference took place. The name Lakshmi Mukti triggered traditional associations of the wife or young bride as Lakshmi, the goddess of wealth, bringing prosperity to the house she is sent to—as is seen in the frequently used term, *grihlakshmi* or 'lakshmi of the house'. Mukti means freedom—so the whole phrase may be taken as a plea to set free the lakshmi of the house.

Sharad Joshi had urged husbands to transfer some of the money from their land to women in the family. Instead, the men of Vitner actually gave portions of the land itself to their wives. The amount was not specified. Each man was supposed to give according to his capacity, the minimum being one acre. The maximum so far has been six acres. Every village which achieved 100 cases of Lakshmi Mukti, or failing that, 80 percent of whose landholders were women, was awarded the title of Jyotiba village. Vitner was awarded this title in 1990, for having made the maximum transfers. A photograph of then prime minister V. P. Singh handing over the award to Shubhatai Raisingh in the village square, flanked by the other panchayat members, hangs—framed—in the gram panchayat office.

What does the transfer of land in her name actually bring to a woman? Does it only add to her work? Who looks after the crop? Who sees to the sale of the produce? Who keeps the money from the sale? Yashodabai Vitthal Patil was given one acre of land in 1989 by her in-laws, who are Sanghatana followers. Yashodabai has been living with her in-laws since her husband died 15 years ago, when her youngest child was still in her womb. Recently when the family decided to split up, Yashodabai was given all of her husband's share of four acres on which she now cultivates sugarcane.

Yashodabai herself sees to the sowing, irrigating, harvesting and even the selling of the cane. The crop is sold in nearby Shirpur, where she proceeds once a year to negotiate with the buyers. As she cannot read or write, two of her sons—one in Class X, the other in Class XII, accompany her to help with the calculations. Yashodabai is grateful to the Sanghatana for giving her a sense of her own *takat* (strength). Were it not for the Sanghatana, she says, she would be left helpless, dependent on her in-laws for food and shelter. She fears her in-laws might have thrown her out of the house in the latest conflict within the family, had she not had the one acre to her name already.

Arch Sanghatana supporter Ghanshyam Patil has made over all his six acres to his wife. His is a special case though: his wife says he has never known how to farm, right from the beginning. In their case, she supervises everything on the land, while he goes to the town to buy fertilisers and to sell the produce. The money from the transactions goes to her; she manages the accounts in the family, as Ghanshyam is too busy with Sanghatana work. Ironically, it is Ghanshyam who keeps a record of the postal accounts of Vitner's women, including that of his wife, into whose account he puts Rs 50 every month.

We sit overlooking three acres of banana crop, eating ripe bananas plucked straight off her trees. Vimlabai owns three acres, her husband another three. Right now the adjoining field, her husband's, is standing tall with young banana trees. The bananas are still young, very green and unripe. Vimlabai and her husband, Gokul, help each other in bringing in the other's harvest. Both decide what crop to sow in the field. If Vimlabai does not agree with her husband, she goes ahead and plants what she wants to—on her land. As the harvesting of crops such as beans and okra is traditionally women's work, she supervises the *mazoori* (daily-wage labourers), squatting together in the fields to pull the beans off the vines. He avoids such work. This last is said with a little smile. On the other hand, Gokul tills both the fields with the oxen, while she sows and plants in the wake of the plough. Banana is a difficult crop to cultivate. The sowing itself is back-breaking work, as every plant has to be individually planted. Then the banana takes a year and a half to ripen, so that one must have enough resources to subsist on between crops.

Vimlabai appears very well-informed on agricultural matters. Gokul shows me a bill for the new pump she has installed in her field; it has cost Rs 1,000. He will see to the care and operation of the pump, while Vimlabai takes care of the bullocks.

'Have the acres in your name made a difference to you?' I ask Vimlabai. 'To your relationship with your husband?'

'No, none whatsoever.'

'Now that you have money in your hands, does it not mean an increased mobility?'

'Well yes, now I can go to my parent's place or to Chopda, whenever I feel like it.'

'So it has made a difference then?'

'No, not really. I was free to do that even before the land was made in my name.'

Vimlabai has a bank account in Wadki, where her husbands deposits the money in her name. But he did that even before the transfer, so it's made no difference.

'The transfer has made no difference in your personal life then?'

'None.'

Gokul, who has been listening silently and impatiently all this while, can finally hold himself back no longer. 'Why don't you ask her the right question, the *mool* [root] question,' he bursts out. 'Ask her what she says to me when we have a fight!'

'What do you say?' I ask.

Vimlabai blushes, looks away, and will not answer.

'I'll tell you,' Gokul says. 'She says, "What do I care where you go now, the land is in my name, you can go where you like."'

Vimlabai begins to laugh helplessly, acknowledging the truth of what has just been said. Gokul too is laughing, shaking his head at me and saying, 'See? you must know what to ask.'

The magic right question is not needed though, when talking to Susheelabai. A member of the panchayat, she is a gutsy spitfire of a woman, one of the star performers the night at Anjubai's.

'Do you want land made over in your name?' I ask.

'MAAA!' is her reply, this dialect's equivalent of 'What do you think? You bet I do!'

Cautiously this time, I say I've heard that it makes no difference. Does it make it a difference?

I am re-greeted with the now-familiar 'MAAA!'

'Why should it make a difference?'

'Because that way I will not be dependent on my sons, or on my husband.'

She turns to her husband and says, amid much laughter, 'You can go if you like, I've got my land.'

'Will the money be in your name?'

'Of course it will.'

Rajubai is engaged in scrubbing the tiled floor of her new home, when I enter. We bend over the tiles together, watching as the intricate pattern begins to show through at last. Rajubai is trying to persuade her husband to expedite the land transfer. Right now, her father-in-law owns all six acres. The land will only become her husband's on the death of his father—she is suggesting he expedite matters during his father's lifetime. They have three daughters, two of whom are already married. Since the third will also soon be married and go away to another's house, she is urging him to make all the land over in her name—as she would be completely defenceless and alone, were anything to happen to him.

Vitner has been much lauded in the national press as a model village in terms of women's property rights. There are stories of how a woman can now offer a snack of nimbu-pani and bananas off 'her' land, and as we have seen, women do not have to kowtow to their husbands, confident in the assurance of financial security. But Vitner also seems to have lost some degree of innocence in all the media hype. The traditional songs—of harvest, of marriages and funerals, of mourning and rejoicing—which have been according to occasion for centuries, appear to have suffered with the 'discovery' of Vitner. On a first visit, the sarpanch's husband, Dashrath Raisingh, urges some women to sing a few songs for the *shahri baika* (city woman), just as they have sung for all the shahri baika who have visited them thus far. They are clearly aware of the fascination that these songs hold for the 'city women' and are willing to sing them regardless of season or occasion. Detractors point out that the rosy picture of Vitner, the panchayat and the Lakshmi Mukti—painted by the press—is not entirely valid. Gopal Guru writes that 'the Sanghatana has decided to appeal to the man dominating the family . . . for [the] transfer of land under the Lakshmi Mukti programme.'[2] Thus the choice and quantity of land to be given lies entirely in the husband's hands. What is the difference then between Lakshmi Mukti and land transfers made, albeit to women, to avoid the Land Ceiling Act?

Very little indeed if one compares the case of Shubhatai Raisingh, the Koli sarpanch, and Yamunabai Patil, Gujjar, wife of the biggest landowner and former sarpanch, Ramdas Patil. Shubhatai owns two of her husband's 10 acres, but her husband sees to all matters dealing with the land. Although she works on the field, she does not have any say in what is to be planted, nor does she keep any of the money from the sale of the produce that grows on her two acres. After her husband, it is her son who will see to all these matters. When she dies, the land in her name will pass over to her daughter-in-law—not to her daughter, who has already received her share of the family wealth as dowry when she got married. Bina Agarwal points out that the Sanghatana has not satisfactorily addressed the issue of who the land goes to after the wife. To ignore the daughter's right to her parents' land, is to repeat the cycle of patriarchy, where a son is immediately privileged simply by virtue of his gender.[3]

Like Shubhatai, Yamunabai Patil also has two acres of land to her name. Each of the three daughters-in-law has been given two acres.

'Has the ownership made any difference to your life?'

'What difference should it make?'

'Have you ever been to the fields?'

'No, never.'

'Not even to have a look?'

'Not even to have a look.'

Using my newly acquired strategy, I ask her what she says when she has a fight. 'Nothing,' she says, 'what should I say, where will I go anyway, with all my children?' And then quickly, for fear she has said too much, she adds, 'And besides, when I feel like all of the land is mine anyway, why worry over two acres?'

Yet Shubhatai was one of the 127 women to be 'given' land, for which Vitner received the Jyotiba award, and Yashodabai was 'given' land to circumvent the land-ceiling act, four years before the Lakshmi Mukti programme was implemented.

Indirabai Patil says there is a difference between the two land transfers: the difference lies in making a demand. Where motivated by the need to circumvent land ceilings, a woman has no part to play in the process. Many times she does not even know there is land to her name. All actual financial transactions are in the stranglehold of the husband, so that the mere paper assigning ownership to her makes no difference to her sense of financial (in)security. With the Lakshmi Mukti programme, however, the wife asks for land as her right—her *'hakka'*, she consciously demands that she be made part-owner of the land. This is a *'hakkachi bhakri'* (literally, rightful bread), and so tastes quite different from the bread received out of *daan* (charity, donation), according to Indirabai.

Indirabai says she herself asked for a share from her husband—before the Lakshmi Mukti programme was implemented—when he bought new land, especially as some of her jewellery went into buying it. Indirabai owns three of the 16 acres owned by her husband, Bhanudas. That property is now worth Rs 4 lakhs—money she can keep solely for herself, should she so desire it. Indirabai is lucky to have a husband who respects her wishes. Ashabai Anand Patil, whose mother owns four acres of land in Vitner, is married into the family of a rich landowner in nearby Vadoda. She too would like a piece of land for herself, but is afraid to ask as her husband is 'not of the Sanghatana' so that were she to do so, she would find herself alone, pitted against her husband and in-laws. Ghanshyam Patil's sister, who is also married to a farmer in Vadoda, agrees. Her husband makes about Rs 25 lakhs out of his 135 acres of land, but every time she has suggested he legally make over some of it in her name, he has put her off by saying, 'Why do you need it, aren't we as one?'

The distinction between *daan* and *hakka* becomes a somewhat fine one, when one's husband is not naturally or willingly amenable to a wife's demands or, for that matter, suggestions. For a woman to feel comfortable to make a demand, she must already enjoy some degree of latitude in her home. Shubhatai is grateful that her husband has stopped coming home drunk and beating her, that he has stopped going out with other women. In such a domestic climate, where there is a question of sheer physical survival, the question of demanding one's rights by asking for land appears somewhat unreal. Unfortunately, too, the notion of women's 'rights' appears to have become one with the notion of women owning land. Thus Ghanshyam does not find the fact that women do not wear chappals at all disturbing. Nor is the presence of an all-men sabha seen as an infringement of women's political rights. This double vision allows women like Arunabai to assert confidently that 'Vitner's women have all the *hakkas*.'

The question as to how much the Lakshmi Mukti programme and the panchayat have changed women's perceptions of themselves, is a moot one. The answer depends as much on which are the women one chooses to focus on, as on the measure one uses to record the change—for that there has been a change is indisputable. Shubhatai and Indirabai have both been in positions of power in the same panchayat. Shubhatai clearly enjoys being part of the political body, as does Indirabai. Yet there is an enormous difference of attitude to the question of women's empowerment between the two women. 'When the *devas* [male gods] are unable to cope with the corruption,' Indirabai says, 'they have to send Durga.' Similarly, humans will have to do the same. *'Stri hi shakti ahe'* (Women are the embodiment of power). For Shubhatai, the rationale for an all-women panchayat is that *'Sharad Joshinni sangitle'*—Sharad Joshi asked us to.

As we sit in the temple on the banks of the Tapi, Shubhatai talks of her only daughter who has been home with them for some months now. She is back from her in-laws, as she says they ill-treat her. Shubhatai says she will be sent back to her husband, but only after a little while. Once the in-laws see that their daughter-in-law is being 'used'—*'vapar karto ahe'*—by her parents, they will automatically take her back without a fuss. The term 'vapar' is startling in this context, but Shubhatai finds nothing unusual in referring to the 'use' of a daughter-in-law.

Indirabai recounts several stories of domestic violence when we meet over the course of a long afternoon in her Chopda house. As president of the Samagra Mahila Aghadi in Jalgaon district, the Sanghatana's front for women, she sometimes shames the guilty party by staging a demonstration along with all of her women workers. At other times, she talks personally with lawyers and husbands. She has apparently succeeded in bringing together many rocky marriages by talking to both husband and wife. Indirabai is obviously outspoken. She had not dared to talk in Chandwad, despite the women urging, 'Why are you silent here? You are a great one for talking otherwise.' But in her first meeting in Chopda, she says she publicly called the Shiv Sena *'jativadis'* (communalists).

As soon as one broaches the question to Shubhatai of why women do not—cannot—wear chappals within the village, references are immediately made to covering one's head as a mark of respect in the presence of one's husband and family elders. The difference between covering one's head and between walking bare foot on blistering soil does not appear to strike Sarpanchbai. She says she takes off her chappals in front of her husband as a mark of respect. In fact, once her son became a father himself, she began to be barefoot in his presence as well—so that his sons and future daughters-in-law will treat him with respect in their turn.

Indirabai has blatantly refused to accept the norms her community expects of a *sabhya* (cultured) woman. Her clothes as well as her manner would frequently call forth the ire of prominent members of the Gujjar samaj. She tells of how terrified she was the first time she wore chappals in the village. Later she says she realized 'people accept you for what you are, and no one says anything anymore.' *'Indirabai tar asich ahe'* (Indirabai is like that only). Disregarding the taunts and ridicule, she has refused to recapitulate, despite occasionally coming into conflict with her husband. But instead of ostracizing her forever, the community has now recognized the worth of her work, so that today Indirabai can walk through the village in her short hair and 5-yard saris, in her fancy footwear, stopping to talk to whoever she pleases. She can walk about with strangers, can ride pillion on the motorcycles of unknown men, travelling two weeks in a month, while her sons and daughter manage all the household work, with the help of a maid.

Can it be said then that the involvement of women in the panchayat is largely a farce? That apart from a handful of women like Indirabai, the fact of women participating in the panchayat is meaningless, since fundamental attitudes remain unchanged? Going by the responses of the women of Vitner, evidently not. As Rajubai, not a member but an active Sanghatana worker, points out, the most obvious benefit of women being in the panchayat, has been that women are no longer completely housebound. It has suddenly become legitimate for women to move out of the house because of the panchayat, as the members may say, for instance, 'we would like the women to be present at so-and-so place at this hour' and since it is on work, no one can prevent them from being there.

The sentiment is echoed by Vimlabai, Gokul's wife. She is a shy, friendly woman who prefers to stay in the shadows in the presence of the newcomer, content to let her husband talk on her behalf. When her husband says he will file her papers for her during the next panchayat elections, I turn to her in inquiry. She says she would like to. And although she accompanies the statement with a self-deprecating laugh and a rueful joke about being an *angtha* (an unlettered woman), it is evident that she is serious about becoming a member.

Susheelabai says that becoming a member of the panchayat has brought her no extra respect at home. According to her, those at home have no *kadar* (respect) for the 'cows' at home, even though cows do so much work. For all that, she is pleased to be part of the panchayat. She cites the same reason others have : that where earlier she could not go out of the house, now she can even go into the homes of strangers. Sarpanchbai herself is no exception for all the seeming meekness. Her statements about 'my' panel, and 'my' idea have already pointed to the pleasure she takes in being Sarpanchbai. Shubhatai is a curious blend of diffidence and pride, aware of being unlettered and at the same time deeply conscious of being sarpanch. On the one hand she appears completely dominated by her husband and to comply and agree fully with those traditions that privilege the son over the daughter. And at the same time she obviously relishes being Sarpanchbai and is reluctant to step down from the position to become Shubhatai again.

The transformation in her on being made sarpanch is all the more miraculous in light of the desperation of her earlier circumstances. Her health improved dramatically. The pictures of her taken before coming into office show an emaciated women with tired, lacklustre eyes. In the pictures taken after, she is almost unrecognizable as the same woman. Although she still does not radiate confidence, her face has filled out, her eyes are brighter, she is smiling.

Although she denies that her being sarpanch has had anything to do with the change in her husband's behaviour (vis-à-vis his drinking and violence), that there has been some shift in the dynamics of that relationship is undeniable. The most visible expression of it is that she sits on a chair while he stands, when in the gram panchayat office or while visiting officers outside of Vitner. Several women comment on this fact, some in her presence. Yashodabai looks meaningfully at the husband as she says, *'Mazhi bai khurchvar baste'* (my lady sits on the chair). Shubhatai smiles.

These above observations are intended to draw attention to the difficulty involved in any enterprise that seeks to settle on one definitive unichrome 'answer' to what is essentially a process, and not a fixed object at all. Anthropologists Jeffrey and Jeffrey explain how 'the system of male privilege, status and property operates not only in the interests of men, but also of women. Women are promised benefits, so that they have a stake in the prevailing social order.'[4] Other anthropologists, notably Gloria Goodwin Raheja and Kirin Narayan, also point out that subservience and resistance, strength and submission, form part of the paradoxical nature of women's experience in India. Thus Susheelabai can cuttingly, furiously, ridicule husbands and mothers-in-laws, can beat them with imaginary sticks, raising her sari high up on her thighs, while all around her raucous laughter rises up in great waves. It is no wonder Gokulbhau does not like these nightly sessions, where the women strictly reserve the right to admittance. Lying outside under a shining sky, watching Scorpio and Orion stretched wide across its expanse, I listen to Vimlabai tell me that Gokulbhau does not like her to participate in these sessions, and so she does not. Gokulbhau calls out that it is all lies, that she is lying and turns over on his side to settle into sleep once more. Vimlabai and I look at each other in the moonlight and laugh silently to each other.

It is this same duality of women's subservience and resistance that does not let Ghanshyam's daughter, Sulochana, openly voice her discontent at her marriage, but allows her to talk confidently of the education she will give to her children, be they boys or girls. Her daughter will definitely have a job, she says. There are other pockets of resistance. A young girl says she will not address her husband as *'aho'* (the respectful term of address for a husband, the calling of his name being considered a sign of disrespect). Instead she will call him by his name, 'of course'. Only *ashikshit* (uneducated) women call their husbands 'aho' The final word belongs to Radhubai. 'People say the men of Vitner are like women . . . let them.'

NOTES

1. Gail Omvedt, The Farmers' Movement in Maharashtra', in Ilina Sen, ed., *A Space Within the Struggle*, (Delhi : Kali for Women; 1990)
2. Gopal Guru, 'Shetkari Sanghatana and the Pursuit of Laxmi Mukti', *Economic and Political Weekly*, (11 July 1992)
3. Bina Agarwal, *A Field of One's Own*, (Delhi : Oxford University Press, 1994)
4. Roger Jeffrey and Patricia Jeffrey, 'Killing My Heart's Desire', in Nita Kumar, ed., *Women as Subjects : South Asian Histories*, (Calcutta : Stree, 1994)

CONCLUSION

Bishakha Datta

'They expect us to behave like women but think like men.'

The experiences of 12 all-women panchayats in Maharashtra have been detailed in this study. Specifically, this has meant

(i) documenting the experiences of the two earliest known panchayats—at Nimbut (1963) and Mauje Rui (1984), both in Pune district

(ii) recording and analysing the experiences of seven recent all-women panchayats formed in 1989 at Bhende Khurd and Ralegan Siddhi, both in Ahmednagar district; Nimbgaon Bhogi and Brahmanghar, both in Pune district; Salod and Erangaon, both in Amravati district; and Yenora in Wardha district

(iii) studying in greater detail and critically evaluating the experiences of three recent all-women panchayats, also formed in 1989, at Bitargaon in Solapur district; Metikheda in Yavatmal district; andVitner in Jalgaon district

All these panchayats represent attempts by rural women to carve out a political space that will enable them to place their needs, concerns and priorities on the political agenda. The experiences of these women—often their first taste of political power—throw up certain patterns, issues and concerns.

These have implications for the larger issue of women's political participation and are summarized here.

The conclusion is informally divided into four ctions:

(*i*) analyses the formation of these panchayats;

(*ii*) explores the programmes taken up by them;

(*iii*) studies patterns of participation;

(*iv*) examines their impact in terms of empowerment.

FORMATION

How were these panchayats formed?

Three distinct patterns underlie the formation of these 12 panchayats. In some—Nimbut, Mauje Rui, Nimbgaon Bhogi and Bitargaon—women themselves decided to form panchayats. In Bitargaon, a spirited woman, Satyabhama 'Nani' Lawand, took the initiative and got the endorsement of male village elders. In Mauje Rui, the water crisis prompted Padmavati Kare to stand for election. 'The men would make sympathetic noises but they wouldn't lift a finger to help us,' she says. 'In two decades of Panchayati Raj, we had just two or three wells. It made me really angry. That's how I came to stand for elections—I knew I'd do better.' In others—Bhende, Ralegan and Brahmanghar—panchayats were formed not as a result of demands from women, but at the behest of men. Sugar baron Namdeo Nawle set up a 'puppet' women's panchayat in Bhende to maintain his hold on local political institutions. In Ralegan Siddhi, bringing women to power became one aspect of reformer Anna Hazare's efforts to transform his village. Brahmanghar's men decided to field a women's panel to avoid factions and preserve village unity. The five Shetkari Sanghatana panchayats—Salod, Erangaon, Yenora, Metikheda and Vitner—were formed on the spontaneous initiative of local, often male, activists responding to the Sanghatana's 1986 call for rural women to enter politics. In Yenora, Sanghatana MLA Vasant Borde took the initiative; local male activists started the process in Salod and Erangaon; in Metikheda, activists Maiah and Chandrakant Wankhede were catalysts. Only in Vitner did a woman activist, Indirabai Patil, take the lead in forming a women's panchayat.

Whatever the pattern may be, one constant is evident: the women's panchayats could not have been formed without the support—direct or indirect—of male leaders or elders. This finding is consistent with activist Madhu Kishwar's assertion that 'a necessary precondition for women's mobilization is the general and usually prior mobilization of the men in the rural community.'[1]

What were the modes through which these panchayats came to power?

About two-thirds of these panchayats came to power unopposed, that is there was no opposing panel and hence no election; only four actually fought elections. All the villages initially tried to avoid elections—so that women would not have to face political abuse and calumny. 'Women are reluctant to contest because of violence, murkiness and potential character assassination,' says Shetkari Sanghatana activist Saroj Kashikar who became an MLA in 1990.[2]

Elections were less preferred also because they typically divide women into rival political factions—and impede their formation as a united political group with common needs and interests. 'Women will not unite in a two-party village,' explains Metikheda's Chandrabhau Patil. 'They will go with their parties.'

Elections could be avoided in the more politically homogenous villages, where the entire village votes as a bloc or takes direction from one political leader. For example, in Bitargaon, the village traditionally votes for the Congress and takes political direction from influential landowner Dadasaheb Patil. Thus they agreed to elect the women, unopposed. In Mauje Rui, funnily enough, an opposing panel withdrew, fearing they would be labelled eunuchs if they lost to a women's panel.

Village concerns that women would face abuse and slander were borne out where women fought elections. In Metikheda, for instance, panel leader Maiah Wankhede was slandered for having short hair. The panel was called *'taklya randya'* (bald women) by the opposition; underlying this was the powerful cultural association between short hair and widow status. Other election strategies that favour men more than women were used at Metikheda. These include liquor (men were given free liquor against guarantees of their wives' votes); family pressure (a concocted letter from a tribal urged his wife not to contest elections); offers of money (which women lack access to); and political institutions, which men control (the opposition had links with the police). The negative impact of such political realities has prompted some activists to question the need for women to participate in politics. 'Are we training women to adjust to adversary politics or to change the political scenario?' asked Meena Galliara of the Tata Institute of Social Sciences during an interview.

How and who were the women chosen to be on the panchayat?

Panchayat members were chosen through an informal system of proportional representation. Each village has different caste-based bastis or colonies. One representative was put on the panel from each basti, including the dalit, backward-class and adivasi bastis.

Literate women were typically preferred, except in Bitargaon, where all village women—including the women's panchayat—is illiterate. Educated women perform better in local government, concludes Hazel D'Lima in her 1980 study of women in Panchayati Raj institutions.[3] She notes that women's education depends not so much on caste, class, income, as on the educational status of her husband or father.

Age was another visible criterion for selecting women candidates. Typically, older women over 40 were given precedence. 'How could we select someone very old or a very young girl and sit and talk with her?' asks Bitargaon's sarpanch. 'Both wheels should be comparable, only then will the cart run well.' D'Lima points out that the average age of women in local government is 45 years. Older women, she says, are allowed greater mobility, face less sexual slander, do not have the workload of young women, or can assign their workload to their daughters-in-law. Thus they have more time for political work.[4]

The sarpanch was typically chosen from the rural political elite. For instance, Brahmanghar's sarpanch, Pushpalata Dhumal, comes from one of the wealthiest families in the village. In Bhende, sugar baron Namdeo Nawle's daughter-in-law was made sarpanch. In Nimbgaon, landowning Usha Badhe initiated the panchayat and led it as sarpanch.

This finding supports those of other studies of village panchayats. One of the biggest inadequacies of village panchayats, including these, is that they replicate rural power structures and deeply embedded patterns of dominance and inequality. In a 1990 study, M. Shiviah and K. B. Srivastava report that 87 percent of villagers surveyed in Karnataka, 60 percent in Gujarat, and 38 percent in Rajasthan perceived gram panchayats as instruments of the dominant castes; they also felt panchayats strengthened the power bases of dominant castes.[5] This feature—seen in many of the all-women panchayats—has implications for the efficacy of panchayats as institutions of self-government.

Metikheda was the sole panchayat that radically subverted existing power structures in favour of more equitable ones. Although sarpanch Maiah Wankhede, an urban-born activist, forms part of the political elite—since urban settlers are typically seen as rural elite—other members come from marginal dalit and tribal communities. Disenfranchisement, rather than literacy—which automatically benefits elites who have greater access to education—seemed to be the key criterion in this selection. Although this can be seen as an exercise in proportional representation in a tribal-dominated village, it is the first time these communities are being given a political voice in Metikheda.

PROGRAMMES

What programmes did the women's panchayats take up?

One of the main reasons for encouraging women to enter politics is the feminist expectation that 'the personal will become the political' that is, that women will project their own experiences, problems and concerns onto the political platform as unmet needs and priorities. Women's needs are often considered to fall outside the purview of traditional politics. This has changed to a large extent; the women's movement has redefined the conventional idea of 'politics', bringing into the public, formal, political domain issues which were earlier located in a private, informal, apolitical domain. Despite this, women's voices—articulating their needs and priorities—still remain unheard in political decision-making and development planning. Women's panchayats offer a chance to visibilize women's concerns.

'One can clearly see that the programmes undertaken by women's panchayats are need-oriented and ecologically sustainable,' writes activist Chetna Galla.[6] Women also conceptualize basic needs quite differently from men. 'If you make two groups and ask them to devise programmes, women will think of water and latrines, while men will talk of roads and buses,' said Anil Singh of Voluntary Action Network of India (VANI) at a 1994 workshop on Panchayati Raj held at Sevagram, Wardha.

Four of the 12 panchayats we studied gave *first* priority to the issue of water scarcity—an unmet need since women are responsible for collecting water. While Mauje Rui's panchayat was formed specifically to address this problem, Bitargaon's panchayat has got a Rs 6 lakh water supply scheme for the drought-prone village—the elevated, concrete water tank is now a prominent village landmark. Vitner's panchayat has succeeded in getting a huge water tank, which dominates the village square, and has put taps in every basti. Says panchayat member Rukmabai, 'I do not have to rush early morning and walk distances for water. For the first time in my life, I can take morning tea with relief.'[7]

In Metikheda, water supply has increased threefold and marginal communities finally have access to water. Eight new community taps and 100 new private taps have been installed, water supply has shot up from one to three hours everyday, and the quantum of water increased from 40,000 cu.l. to 120,000 cu.l. each day. The provision of water to marginal groups which had earlier been denied access must be seen as a major challenge to existing power structures. Water scarcity is so endemic in Maharashtra's villages that it would require an estimated Rs 3,000 crores to solve it. A male colleague suggests a cheaper way to solve this crisis: elect only women's panchayats in all villages for the next five years!

Several of the panchayats built *extra* schoolrooms so that higher classes could be added. This has had a favourable impact on daughters, who will not be sent outside the village to study. Panchayat women have been assertive in increasing educational facilities in every single village we went to. In Brahmanghar, women built a road to the school so that their children would not slip and fall in the rains. They also demanded and got an additional teacher. And in Bitargaon, the dilapidated tin school—where children got wet in the monsoons—has been upgraded to a concrete building. In Mauje Rui, where classes were earlier held under a tree, eight classrooms have been built. In Vitner, with the construction of new rooms, the school has been extended to class seven. In Nimbgaon, the school has been extended from class seven to class ten, which means more girls can study up to class ten now! In fact all these initiatives have benefitted girls who are not sent outside the village to study.

Panchayats also brought in *community toilets* and *smokeless chulhas*—to address the issues of sanitation and fuel, but these have been uniformly unsuccessful. Although community toilets are need-based schemes, in village after village, women refuse to enter these 'dirty toilets.' Similarly, they refuse to use smokeless chulhas, which stand like discontented white elephants in most kitchens. Metikheda's Maiah Wankhede attributes the failure of smokeless chulhas to basic design defects, which allowed water to re-enter the house through the chimney pipe. 'In my pipe, because of the water, there used to be frogs,' she says. 'They used to shit in that and an awful smell used to come.'

In one case, Metikheda, the panchayat's philosophy located itself in addressing *women's* needs to the extent that it even financed and repaired taps in 24 hours. Frequent breakdowns, delayed repairs and poor maintenance only burdens women, says the panchayat. 'For 15 days there is no water. We had decided women should have no water problem. So even if there is a pump failure, within 24 hours we manage it,' says the sarpanch. 'We are the only gram panchayat with this philosophy.'

All these examples conclusively prove that even where women have come to power at the behest of men, they have managed to place their own needs on the political agenda.

Did women panchayats use formal mechanisms or informal systems to meet these needs?

Most programmes—water, electricity, toilets, smokeless chulhas—were brought in by tapping existing government schemes. Panchayat members often met local political leaders—notably MLAs—to lobby for schemes. In one instance, Bitargaon sarpanch Nani Lawand denied a visiting MLA tea to make her point about water scarcity. 'I told him we would have given him tea but there was no water.'

Many women's panchayats used similar, informal, innovative methods. In Vitner, the panchayat told women to let loose their cattle on 52 acres of common property that was being encroached on. The panchayat has now reclaimed the land and turned it into a community orchard; proceeds form part of the panchayat fund. Similarly, in Metikheda the panchayat led starving animals into the jungle to graze during a severe drought. Even though this was illegal, the administration took no action—they feared that resultant publicity would make other villages do the same!

In Brahmanghar, 22 women marched to the Block Development Officer and demanded he sanction an extra teacher for the school; the new teacher has started taking classes. And the panchayat—in cooperation with the Mahila Mandal—ensured that one woman came from every house to dig the 70-foot road to the school. Any house that didn't send a woman was fined Rs 25. 'Everyone came,' says sarpanch Pushpalata Dhumal. 'Even elderly women came and put one stone.' This collective spirit is evident when we recreate the 'dig' for a photo-session.

Brahmanghar's sarpanch reports that it is easier for a women's panchayat to take advantage of formal mechanisms. 'Everywhere it is known that this is an all-women panchayat. So if we go to the Panchayat Samiti, they give us more attention. So the work gets done faster.' This experience is not universal. More universal is the experience of using formal mechanisms first, informal and pressure mechanisms when these do not work.

It is interesting to note that these informal, pressure mechanisms were often devised by women themselves—not by external agencies such as NGOs. Is this partly because women, who lack familiarity with formal political processes, tend to create their own informal political spaces, mechanisms and systems to ensure they can participate effectively? If so, can this be seen as a vital survival mechanism which has the potential to transform the nature of politics?

Is there a difference between the programmes introduced by women's panchayats and traditional, male-dominated panchayats?

Although it is tempting to hold women's panchayats solely responsible for addressing women's needs, there is actually little difference in the formal schemes implemented by women's and 'mixed' panchayats. For instance in Tembhurna, a village neighbouring Bitargaon, a male-dominated panchayat added rooms to the existing school, repaired handpumps and roads, and acquired a primary health centre. In neighbouring Mitkalwadi too, a similar panchayat completed a tapwater project, repaired handpumps and brought electricity and better roads.

A 1990 study shows that 33 percent of villagers surveyed in Gujarat said the 'one work that attracted their gram panchayat's attention' was education. Another 33 percent of the same villagers said the 'one work attracting the panchayat's attention' was drinking water supply.[8] In Rajasthan and Karnataka too, villagers said the panchayat gave greatest priority to drinking water supply. Most of these were traditional, male-dominated panchayats. These findings refute the common expectation that only women will address women's needs.

This phenomenon can partially be explained by the introduction of Jawahar Rozgar Yojana. Introduced in 1989 and today the single-biggest source of annual panchayat funds, JRY has homogenized development to some extent. All JRY expenditures have to be routed through the Panchayat Samiti—which mainly sanctions schemes involving construction. Since 'water supply schemes' and 'education' both require construction, panchayats routinely apply for such schemes under JRY funds. Thus, at a programme level, there is often little difference between women's panchayats and male-dominated panchayats.

What is the advantage, then, of women's panchayats?

Despite the similarities between some women's and mixed panchayats, rural women strongly believe that their needs are not addressed by traditional political structures. 'We completed the tapwater scheme,' says Kamal Mastud, a dalit member of Bitargaon's panchayat. She points out that villagers had been demanding the scheme for years. 'Men wouldn't have done the kind of work we did.' There is a similar perception in Metikheda. Says village matriarch, Parvati Jaiswal, 'I've spent 60 years in this village. Nothing had been done before the women came to power. Nothing.'

Again, this could partly be explained by the JRY, whose start in 1989 coincided with the start of most of the women's panchayats, assuring these panchayats access to constant funding. However, this is just one of several factors influencing the performance of women's panchayats.

Villagers point out that women are able to accomplish more simply because they are less prone to corruption. Earlier panchayats did mobilize funds and grants, say villagers, but they didn't show any work in return. Corruption is acknowledged to be so endemic to Panchayati Raj institutions that Rajiv Gandhi once estimated that only 15 paise out of each rupee ultimately reaches beneficiaries.

Except Nimbgaon Bhogi's sarpanch Usha Badhe, all the other women sarpanches were viewed as extremely honest. (Of panchayat members, sarpanches have the highest opportunity for corruption, since the panchayat account is jointly handled by the sarpanch and the gram sevak.) Is this because women are essentially 'purer' than men, as some activists suggest? Or is it just that women, who are unfamiliar with political mechanisms, do not know how to take advantage of opportunities for corruption?

This single feature—an absence of corruption—sets all-women panchayats apart from other panchayats. Vitner's women say that earlier panchayats were interested in monetary gains; they would opt for construction activities because they could get commissions on them. Even Vitner's men agree with this assessment, saying 'they never undertook a project until they were sure it would be profitable.'[9] This is a universal phenomenon at all political layers: a political position is seen as an opportunity for award of contracts, not as an opportunity for community service.[10]

While all the women's panchayats are free of corruption, only Metikheda has actively fought corruption at other levels of Panchayati Raj. This is mainly because of the vigorous leadership of its urban-born sarpanch. Two gram sevaks were suspended for corruption; the panchayat members routinely monitor weights, material, and expenditures. In one case, they bought toilet seats themselves and proved that the engineer's bills for the seats had been inflated!

Do women's panchayats benefit the entire village? Or do women's panchayats only benefit women?

Men like Metikheda's Marutrao Atram believe the women's panchayat has contributed not just to women's development, but to the overall development of the village. 'For 40 years, nobody had paid attention to the issue of water,' he says. 'But nine women were elected, and the water problem became much less.' Underlying his statement is the perception that scarcities of water and other 'women's problems' affect the entire village population.

Several activists hold that the division between women's issues and general issues is an artificial one. 'Each issue concerns women as it does men and has a women's perspective to it,' write Nandita Shah and Nandita Gandhi.[11] A report of a workshop on grassroots democracy cautions that 'creating a myth about "women's issues" should not mean leaving women out of important committees that deal with other vital matters for rural development.'[12] This myth has often saddled women with responsibility only for 'women and children's issues' and left them out of decision-making on other, wider issues.

The wider way in which women's panchayats empower village women is in giving them a collective voice. A sole female member will hardly speak in front of male panchayat colleagues; attempts to speak raise comments like 'Oh, so you're trying to become a leader.'[13] This lack of participation—seen at all layers, up to Parliament—often turns women in politics into a 'silent minority.' But there is safety in numbers; Drude Dahlerup explains that women entering the political system are in a stronger position when there is a 'critical mass' of 25–30 percent women in a political body.[14] They can now intervene and be heard in a male-dominated body. A women's panchayat—with a critical mass of 100 percent—represents a greater chance to be heard.

This is of significance to women outside the political system. 'If women are elected, then women can go to them and ask for help without feeling afraid,' says Gangaben Solanki, a Bombay-based dalit activist. 'Suppose there is a dispute. The woman feels hesitant coming before a group of men... she cannot speak freely.' Although Gangaben is talking in the context of caste panchayats—which arbitrate marital and family disputes—her point holds for gram panchayats.[15] Perhaps it is this vital understanding that compelled the 1974 Committee on the Status of Women to recommend establishing statutory women's panchayats in villages as an integral part of Panchayati Raj.[16]

Do the benefits of women's panchayats reach all women?

The impact that the panchayat has had on women's lives seems to be mediated by their caste and class position to some extent. In some villages like Vitner, Bhende Khurd, Nimbgaon Bhogi and Brahmanghar, the dalit member insists that the women's panchayat has not benefitted her community in any way.

'How has the panchayat benefitted us?' asks Alka Chavan, the dalit member of Brahmanghar's panchayat. 'There has been no benefit till today.' Although the panchayat has built an extra room in her house, she feels it has not provided other necessities: street lighting for the dalit colony like the rest of the village; water connections in the house; a tar road from the main village road to their colony. 'If men came on the panchayat, they would do more work—quicker,' she grumbles. Alka Chavan's discontent is partly born out of being on a panchayat where her voice is often not heard. Although she says the villagers do not discriminate on the basis of caste, she clearly feels there is little common ground between the upper-caste Dhumals and the dalit Chavans: they have different problems. Her problems get submerged in the bargain. 'I keep telling the sarpanch about the road, electricity,' she says. 'She keeps saying it will be done. But it isn't done.' As a result, she rarely attends panchayat meetings.

Similar discontents are voiced in other villages, particularly in Bhende, where a women's panchayat remote-controlled by a male sugar baron, has completely denied development benefits to the dalits who form 80 percent of the village. Even the 'Below Poverty Line' list—which determines who gets access to poverty-alleviation schemes—is stacked with the names of affluent families, rather than dalits. This is merely an extreme case showing how panchayat benefits do not always reach everyone; they are typically mediated by class and caste.

Are women's panchayats able to address all women's issues?

In Metikheda, women—led by the panchayat members—successfully mobilized around the priority issue of fodder (by illegally letting animals graze in the forest during a drought), but were unable to tackle the equally important issue of alcoholism. At a community meeting on alcoholism, not one woman dared speak, fearing retribution from her husband.

Why do panchayats feel empowered to solve some issues (albeit through informal structures) but powerless to tackle others (also informally)? Metikheda's fodder issue could be solved because of full community support; alcoholism received the limited support of women. Kishwar writes that women's work is 'acceptable to men only as long as they can see the immediate benefits to the family without challenging the power of men.'[17] This is validated in the case of Metikheda.

Writers like Carolyn Moser and Maxine Molyneux distinguish between two categories of women's needs—'practical' and 'strategic'.[18] Practical needs derive from the gender division of labour—looking after children, filling water, cooking for the family and so on. Women's attempts to meet these needs—by securing access to water, land, fuel, and so on—benefits the family without confronting male interests. Strategic needs, on the other hand, arise from women's attempts to confront this traditional package: gender roles, division of labour, male dominance and privilege. Women's attempts to meet these needs—by fighting rape, unequal wages, alcoholism, domestic violence—usually confront male interests and are resisted. Typically, it is much easier to address women's practical needs than to address women's strategic interests.

Feminists have often wondered if the increase in the number of women entering politics will lead to more egalitarian gender relations. Although this is a long-term goal, the above example shows how difficult it is for panchayats to secure gender justice. However, there are examples of panchayats succeeding in this respect. West Bengal's panchayats have taken up issues like dowry which relate to women's strategic interests; one panchayat in Rajasthan has even supported a woman's bid to leave an abusive husband. Thus panchayats—in their role as village leaders—do have the potential to use this leadership to transform gender relations, albeit in a limited way.

PARTICIPATION

What are the patterns of participation in women's panchayats?

Most panchayats divide the workload among members—in Metikheda and Bitargaon, members were allocated portfolios. The Bitargaon panchayat has five portfolios: construction, education, health, prohibition and miscellaneous. But other than the sarpanch, only two members seemed to be cognisant of portfolio responsibilities.

Despite the presence of such formal structures, the sarpanch shoulders the workload in almost all villages. This is partly due to the structure of Panchayati Raj, which gives only the sarpanch—and the gram sevak— power over panchayat funds. Even otherwise, the sarpanch is inevitably the most vocal member at meetings, and the only member with some knowledge of Panchayati Raj mechanisms. This has led to a somewhat centralized style of functioning—in which other members do not 'effectively participate' in the panchayat. In some villages, the sarpanch is effectively the panchayat. This then is one of the central paradoxes of these panchayats: it throws up strong women leaders as well as centralized styles of leadership. But there is some evidence that women do wish to participate: in Nimbgaon, a highly centralized style of functioning has led four women to resign from the panchayat. All of them say they were not consulted on development and financial matters.

Dalit women were most notable in their lack of participation—if measured through attendance at meetings. Perhaps this is because of distance. Brahmanghar's Alka Chavan says her dalit basti is too far from the gram panchayat office, where meetings are held. Or perhaps this is because of caste dynamics. Either way, groups that offer training in Panchayati Raj need to seriously address the issue of power dynamics among women. These dynamics will have to be challenged if dalit women are to be empowered to participate more effectively.

Vitner's dalit member, Dwarkabai, guffaws when asked if she attends meetings. 'Who has the time to attend meetings at ten o'clock in the morning?' she asks. In other villages too, women, regardless of caste, say they cannot drop work in the fields—which are often an hour's walk from the village—to attend meetings. Women have little control over meeting timings, since the gram sevak's mandatory presence means meetings must be held during office hours. But this does effectively inhibit participation. 'Women's primary role and duty as a wife and mother restricts their participation in the public sphere,' write Shah and Gandhi. 'Most often women bear a double burden of work in the household and in the workplace. Political activity would become a triple burden.'[19]

What are the patterns of participation in panchayat meetings?
Meetings are legally required to be held once a month; registers showed that these were generally held at most villages, barring Nimbgaon Bhogi and Bhende Khurd. We attended a June 1994 panchayat meeting in Bitargaon, which was led by the gram sevak. The women's participation was neither entirely invisible nor entirely effective. Women thumbprinted their attendance and cursorily discussed how to allocate money available for dalit students. Each woman contributed at least one comment.

'The expenditure must be equal for all.'

'We must provide that which is not available at home.'

'One uniform costs Rs 100. Rs 1,000 isn't enough for 32 students.'

But there was little of the informed debate and discussion that is traditionally associated with political discourse. The women did not seem very clear about their roles and responsibilities at panchayat meetings—and readily accepted the gram sevak's agenda. This is also seen in the functioning of panchayats in other states. At a Karnataka meeting, for instance, one woman's actions revealed that she believed that her main role was one of putting her signature to the proceedings book.[20]

'These institutions are outside the realm of the traditional experience of women,' writes development planner L. C. Jain.[21] 'The concept, scope, structure, rules and laws governing these institutions, the responsibilities and rights of individual members were not known to an overwhelming majority of the women sufficiently.' This was much the case with all the panchayats we visited.

How informed are panchayat members about Panchayati Raj?
In Bhende Khurd, members didn't know how many other members there are on the panchayat. In Erangaon, members weren't aware that their terms had ended. In most villages, members knew the panchayat's term (five years), names of fellow members, and programmes they had taken up. They knew what a gram sabha was and that it met twice a year.

In terms of schemes, many had vaguely heard of the Jawahar Rozgar Yojana, a key source of panchayat finance. Many knew that the panchayat collects water, house and electricity tax, although they didn't know the amounts collected. Most knew that panchayat funds come from the Panchayat Samiti and the zilla parishad, although they couldn't specify schemes or amounts. Barring the sarpanch, whose knowledge of panchayat functions is significantly higher, none of the members had any idea what different schemes cost. In Vitner, one member said the school compound cost Rs 8,000, sarpanch Shubhatai said it cost Rs 10,000—while panchayat records indicate that Rs 21,000 was spent. Even in villages which have a 'portfolio' system, individual members were unaware of their portfolio responsibilities. In Bitargaon, Laxmi Karande may know that running the health portfolio means disinfecting the well, distributing anti-malaria tablets, ensuring gutters are kept clean, and sending the sepoy to fetch a doctor in emergencies. But Naagarbai Kolte, who heads the construction portfolio, has no idea when the water tank was built!

Very few sarpanches, let alone members, had heard of the Seventy-Third Amendment. Only where elections were held in 1995 did members immediately became aware that 33 percent of seats are reserved for women. 'If you ask villagers about the 29 subjects under Panchayati Raj, they know nothing about it,' said health activist N. H. Antia at a 1994 workshop on Panchayati Raj. 'Absolutely nothing.' An interesting contrast emerged in Brahmanghar in this respect. The sarpanch had never heard of the Seventy-Third Amendment and knew none of its provisions. But the mahila mandal head knew many provisions of the State Policy for Women, enacted two years after the amendment. Why is one filtering down to the village level but not the other?

At a 1994 workshop for NGOs, activist Surekha Dalvi of the Mandlik Trust pointed out that even men know little about Panchayati Raj. But in at least one village, Erangaon, women members had not heard of any schemes, while the male member rattled off names of several schemes. Perhaps it is utopian to expect women to know of such matters in their very first term in office. Either way, informing members of Panchayati Raj basics is a priority area for trainers. Is it possible, feasible or at all desirable to endorse governance without information?

What are the factors that constrain effective participation in all-women panchayats?

Several factors constrain effective participation in all-women panchayats. Some of these relate to a patriarchal culture which neither sees women as political entities nor allows them to develop in this direction. When one woman wanted to attend a training camp on Panchayati Raj, her husband asked, 'And who will make the chapatis?'[22] The same cultural standards also prohibit women from seeing themselves as political entities. Other, related factors that constrain participation are: a lack of basic familiarity with politics, political modes, discourse and skills; inconvenient meeting timings that preclude rural working women from attending, let alone participating; and restrictions on women's mobility.

The structures of Panchayati Raj also work to inhibit participation. Although the Seventy-Third Amendment is widely seen as an enabling mechanism, critics point out that there is no provision to transfer financial powers to panchayats. A lack of financial resources and autonomy effectively limits the extent of participation. Bureaucracy is yet another barrier. Metikheda's sarpanch once had to visit Panchayat Samiti offices 70 times to get a single scheme implemented.

Perhaps the most critical constraint to effective participation is illiteracy. Uneducated members cannot read official documents or even amounts on cheques they sign. In 1994, Bitargaon's sarpanch Nani Lawand signed a document asserting that a water-supply scheme had been handed over to the village in a functioning condition. The scheme was not, in fact, functional, but she couldn't read the document. Her signature has led to a dispute between the village and the Maharashtra Water Supply and Sewerage Board over who should take responsibility for repairing the water tank. Panchayat members themselves identify literacy as a critical need. 'We have two eyes,' says Nani. 'The educated have two and a half.' The entire panchayat, which is illiterate, depends upon the gram sevak, who functions as a de facto sarpanch, albeit a benevolent one. Despite being an employee of the state, he sided with the village, rather than the state Sewerage Board on the recent dispute over the water tank.

In Vitner, unschooled sarpanch Shubha Raisingh's dependence on the gram sevak has produced less benign results. She believes the previous gram sevak, taking advantage of her illiteracy, has cheated the panchayat of a lot of money. Although her interpretation is dismissed by others, the incident points to the state of utter dependency and discomfort forced upon women by a lack of basic literacy. Literacy is a basic requirement for panchayats to become independent self-governing bodies.

How do members of all-women panchayats view or interpret their functions?

Given their fledgling status and their non-traditional nature, it is essential not to burden women's panchayats with too many expectations. It is realistic to expect that women, in their very first term, would interpret their roles as panchayat members somewhat narrowly. This was much the case with the panchayats we visited.

Barring panchayats backed by the Shetkari Sanghatana, all the panchayats limited their role to getting government schemes sanctioned for their villages. At their widest, panchayats have been seen not just as bodies to implement development schemes, but as institutions of self-governance that would effectively control, transfer and direct community resources. Few of the women's panchayats were able to envision, let alone start implementing this agenda. Barring Metikheda, which has interpreted its functions widely enough to include fodder, alcoholism, and corruption, none of the panchayats we visited was able to redefine its role beyond the officially defined one.

In Brahmanghar, for instance, members say collecting firewood is a critical problem. But the panchayat does not dream of taking up this issue. Women clearly see themselves more as implementers of government schemes than as representatives of the community in this respect. Is this because of a lack of knowledge, inadequate opportunities for mobilization, or just the heavy weight of officialdom, which with its paraphernalia of rules, regulations, minutes, agendas and meeting rituals ensures that its own needs are perpetually served?

There is evidence of gram panchayats elsewhere being able to widen their role beyond narrow, official definitions. West Bengal's panchayats have been involved in dowry, literacy and health campaigns, and have lobbied for equal land rights for women. In rural Rajasthan, a gram panchayat has supported a woman's decision to leave her husband who was ill-treating her.[23] In Maharashtra's Satara district, a panchayat has started a project on waste-recycling.[24]

It is possible to broaden the scope of these panchayats through formal or informal linkages with other community-based groups. For instance, mahila mandals exist in several of Maharashtra's villages. (Interestingly, mahila mandals are heavily dependent on gram sevikas, just as panchayats depend heavily on gram sevaks.) There is little doubt that both mahila mandals and panchayats would function more effectively if linkages were established between them.

Do panchayat members participate in other political activities?

Even though women formally occupy positions of power, they are not seen as political entities. This is clearly brought out in the case of Bitargaon, where women—including panchayat members—do not attend the gram sabha which is mandatorily held twice a year. Villagers clearly do not feel an all-male gram sabha is an anomaly in a village with a women's panchayat. This is evident from the conversation we had with the otherwise progressive gram sevak.

'Who attends the gram sabha?' we ask.

'Everyone,' he says.

'Everyone?'

'Yes, everyone.'

'Do the men attend?' we specify.

'Yes.'

'The women?'

'No, no.'

Clearly 'everyone' in this context means 'men'—even though women as voters theoretically enjoy equal representation on the gram sabha, which is defined as the adult electorate. Panchayats are held accountable to the gram sabha. This finding is consistent with the experiences of panchayats in other states. A study done in Himachal Pradesh shows that women do not participate in gram sabhas at all. 'Our analysis is that unless the gram sabhas are made strong there is no future for Panchayati Raj bodies,' writes Subhash Mendhapurkar of SUTRA in the study. 'The gram sabhas cannot become strong if women are not involved.'[25]

This is an issue of as much, if not greater, importance as the issue of women's participation as elected members. On the one hand, women are not considered part of the electorate. On the other, they are superficially accepted as political leaders. Is such an artificial situation tenable, sustainable or desirable? NGOs engaged in training initiatives need to address this basic anomaly if genuine conditions for enabling women's political participation are to be created.

EMPOWERMENT

What is the impact of all-women panchayats?

While it is possible to analyse the impact of women's panchayats in terms of the visible outcomes of development, such as water tanks, school buildings, roads, it is much harder to assess their impact in terms of the invisible processes of development. Empowerment is one such invisible process that a women's panchayat is expected to facilitate.

How does one begin to define, let alone measure, empowerment, which is more a multihued process than a unichrome outcome? Can one say that the Metikheda panchayat, by bringing numerous development benefits to the village, has empowered women? Can one see empowerment in Bitargaon, where women are on the panchayat, but not on the gram sabha? Each panchayat has undergone distinct yet differently nuanced processes of empowerment. How does one measure these nuances?

In her analysis of four women's panchayats, activist Galla distinguishes between those which result in 'transformative change' and 'non-transformative change.' Galla, a Sanghatana activist, writes that Sanghatana-backed panchayats in Metikheda, Yenora and Vitner have led to 'transformative change', while a non-Sanghatana panchayat in Ralegan Siddhi has led to 'non-transformative change.'[26] According to her, the outcomes of development are visible in Ralegan, in the form of 'flourishing trees, neatness, water provision.' But the processes of development —measured as 'transformation'—are absent. 'Discussing with the women of the panchayat provides no sense of any transformation of their traditional status.'[27] Although all four villages have taken up roughly the same issues, Galla believes that only the

Sanghatanabacked panchayats have transformed women's lives. According to her, increased access to water is 'transformative' for the women of Metikheda, Vitner and Yenora, whose workload has gone down, but is 'non-transformative' for the women of Ralegan, whose workload has also gone down. The limitations of this analysis are evident.

Galla's analysis takes an unnecessarily narrow, even compartmentalized, view of the simultaneous and interlinked processes and outcomes of development, empowerment and transformation. Can the 'flourishing of trees' and the 'provision of water' in Ralegan not be said to have transformed women's lives at all? Is the transformation of everyday drudges not an adequate transformation? Can transformations be ranked, where some are deemed greater than others? If so, who should rank them other than the subject of these transformations? And are there no linkages between outcomes('flourishing trees') and processes ('transformation of traditional status')?

A broader framework for empowerment emerges from the writing of Ramya Subrahmanian. Subrahmanian points out that the term empowerment is increasingly used by differing constituencies—governments, donors, activists and so on—who develop differing notions of empowerment. She argues that 'the terms, meaning and end-goal of empowerment should ultimately be left to the 'disempowered' groups to decide.'[28] While identifying a range of interventions that can be seen as empowering, she emphasises that 'indicators of women's empowerment can only be developed by women themselves. . . For women, the process by which they learn to sit on a chair, or sign their names, or even opportunities to enhance their mobility are empowering and carry great potential for transformation.'[29] This wider definition of empowerment is used to evaluate the impact that women's panchayats have had on women's lives. This impact is broken down into loose indicators of empowerment, evolved by the women themselves during informal talks.

Social recognition and respect

Right from the first women's panchayat in Nimbut, women pinpoint this as a key indicator of empowerment. 'It was a great honour for me to become sarpanch of an all-women panchayat at a time when Indira Gandhi had not even become the prime minister of India,' says Kamalbai Kakade, who became sarpanch of Nimbut in 1963. Her colleague, Vatsalabai, still remembers the jeep that took her to panchayat meetings in style, the chairs they sat on at meetings, the photographs taken of them, even the unlikely American who came to interview them.

Similarly, Padmavati Kare, who led the Mauje Rui panchayat in 1984, recalls the letter that Indira Gandhi wrote, congratulating her. 'It made my mother-in-law proud of me,' she recalls. For Brahmanghar's Mandakini Dhumal, recognition has taken the form of her brother, 'who came from his village to visit me after reading about it in the papers,' she says.

And in Metikheda, recognition has come from neighbouring villages. The village of Mohda has modelled its water supply scheme after Metikheda's; another village, Khora, put up an all-women panel in the 1995 panchayat elections. 'When we go out and tell people we're from Metikheda we feel proud,' says a villager.

Mobility, awareness and knowledge

Most women refer to increased mobility, awareness and knowledge as a lasting gain. 'I felt good going all the way to Baramati to meet the Block Development Officer,' recalls Kamalbai Kakade. In Vitner, this has had a wider effect: it has become legitimate for other women to move out of the house when the panchayat calls them to discuss something. Vitner's women have also extended the bus to their village. 'Before this, we hardly used to leave this village,' says one woman.

Political status

As has earlier been discussed, although women have been given political power, they are still not seen as political entities. In Brahmanghar, women were asked to form the panchayat to maintain village unity, since they were not seen as political entities. It was expected that men, who are seen as political entities, would fight for political power during the panchayat elections. In most villages, women still do not attend the gram sabha and lack political knowledge.

Ironically, one of the few women who is seen as a political entity is Usha Badhe, sarpanch of Nimbgaon Bhogi from 1989.

Ushabai's record as a sarpanch is shoddy—four women resigned from the panchayat during her tenure, development schemes are conspicuous by their absence, and she is surrounded by charges of corruption. But she is recognized as a political entity in her own right, because she manifests the attributes of a typical male politician.

Ushabai is a member of five committees including the Panchayat Samiti, the Mahila Mandal and the Lok Nyayalaya. One villager refers to her high connections and her political clout. 'The attributes considered necessary for political effectiveness are seen as quintessentially masculine,' points out Maxine Molyneux in this respect.[30]

Family status

It is obviously difficult to measure if political participation has changed this intimate terrain of women's lives. However, the following anecdotes offer some glimpses. Kamal Mastud of Bitargaon insists her husband has stopped drinking after she became a panchayat member. On the other hand, in Metikheda, Pramila Javade's life has not changed along this dimension: her alcoholic husband continues to batter her. In Brahmanghar, a confident Mandakini Dhumal nonchalantly refuses to obey her brother-in-law's repeated orders to bring home the cattle, now! Instead, she calmly carries on talking to us for another hour.

The most visible change in family status is seen in Vitner's Shubha Raisingh, whose husband stopped battering her after she became sarpanch. Her health has improved dramatically. Photos of her taken before coming into office show an emaciated woman with tired, dull eyes. In the pictures taken after, she is almost unrecognizable as the same woman. Although she still does not radiate confidence, her face has filled out, her eyes are brighter, she is smiling. The shift in the power dynamics between Shubhatai and her husband are evident. She sits on a chair, while he stands in the gram panchayat office or when visiting offices outside of Vitner. At the same time, she often allows him to speak on her behalf, formally and informally.

Shubhatai's daily tussles with power and powerlessness embody the dual pattern of subservience and resistance, strength and submission that forms part of the paradoxical nature of women's experience in India.

Identity as women

There is no doubt that women have developed at least a nascent gender consciousness as a result of being on the panchayat. 'If we have to get some work done and we go to the Panchayat Samiti, they give us more attention because we are all women,' says Brahmanghar's Pushpalata Dhumal. 'The work gets done faster.' Several of Brahmanghar's women unequivocally condemn dowry, and talk candidly on subjects like menstruation and infertility. One or two of them even talk of the need for women's land rights without being prompted by us. They not only identify their own needs—lack of a maternity hospital and the absence of economic schemes—but have also started a credit and savings scheme for the village women on their own initiative. The women's panchayat, the credit committee and the mahila mandal work hand in hand and have created a tentative space for Brahmanghar's women. However, this is partly because of an absence of men in the village who have migrated to Bombay for work.

This process matches a range of interventions that Subrahmanian identifies as empowering: enabling access to and control over new economic resources, involving women in identifying their own needs, transforming awareness, building new and collective relationships, and mobilizing around self-defined needs and priorities.[31]

This nascent women's consciousness is prevalent to some extent in all villages. 'Eight women from eight houses listened to me more than they listened to their mother-in-law,' says Nani of Bitargaon. Her colleague expresses it differently. 'Because of the panchayat, women got at least that much time to sit and talk about things, otherwise every day we had to do the same work, at home and in the fields.' At the same time, Bitargaon's women still view dowry and second marriages as traditional, natural, and therefore, correct. In this context, our attempts to bring up issues of sharing housework and land rights justifiably evoked wild, incredulous laughter.

In Vitner, women's consciousness has taken on a somewhat paradoxical edge. The women have land in their own names and keep referring to their rights. On the other hand, they are content to follow a tradition which bars them from wearing chappals, unlike the men, even when their feet burn in the sun. What does it mean that women hold political office and own land in their own name but must take off their chappals before they enter the village?

If there is one area where women's consciousness has had a visible universal impact, it is on women's attitudes to their daughters. 'Now that one has got this experience,' says Brahmanghar's Pushpalata Dhumal, 'one feels the daughter, daughter-in-law, they also should do something.' Attitudes towards daughters have changed in all villages. The ill-effects of their own lack of education have forced panchayat women to understand the importance of educating their own daughters.

Decision-making

As has been noted through the study, being on the panchayat is one way of participating in decision-making. This has had a wider effect to some extent. For instance, Padmavati Kare, who was sarpanch of Mauje Rui's panchayat, is now on the village panchayat, and heads the village mahila mandal. She has just paid a lawyer out of her own pocket to assist a woman whose husband beat and deserted her and thus also informally influences community decisions.

But women still do not participate fully in community decision-making. In Brahmanghar, women still remain excluded from the village's traditional power bases. Women have no representation on the agricultural credit society which arranged financing for a Rs 14 lakh community irrigation scheme. Women have no voice on the traditional caste panchayat which settles village disputes. And neither do any of the women—in their capacity as water-users and agriculturists—attend the urgent meeting held when the lift-irrigation pipe breaks down. 'But they'll discuss fittings and all,' says Parvati Dhumal. 'Why should we go to the meeting?' It is clear then that even though women have been allowed to occupy political space, they are still expected to remain in their place.

Clearly, it is too much to expect that panchayats will completely, and at one stroke, transform women's lives and experiences. Bitargaon's Nani sums up what the overall experience has meant for her. 'The women got so much power,' she explains, 'power so that people obeyed them. The fact that people respected what they said and did pleased the women. That no one drinks now, there is less trouble, that much power, that much comfort in the hearts. That the villagers feel they ought to follow her decisions, that much satisfaction. Earlier, the husbands would never talk gently, now they talk with a little concern. All this means we are more content now.'

Perhaps the biggest indicator of contentment is that many of the women would like to stand for another term; most of these panchayats were dissolved in 1994. In Vitner one woman who was not a panchayat member talks of filing her papers for the next elections. And in Bitargaon, Nani says the same thing in her own earthy style. 'I would like to do this work as long as I live. But even if we don't stand again, this experience will have been enough.'

NOTES

1. Madhu Kishwar, 'Nature of Women's Mobilisation in Rural India', *Economic and Political Weekly*, (24-31 Dec 1988), p.2754
2. Nandita Shah and Nandita Gandhi, *The Quota Question*, Mumbai: Akshara, (1991), p.4
3. Hazel D'Lima, 'The Participation of Women in Local Self-Government', Bombay: Nirmala Niketan College of Social Work, (1984), p.2
4. ibid., 3
5. M. Shiviah and K.B. Srivastava, *Factors Affecting Development of the Panchayati Raj System*, (Hyderabad: National Institute of Rural Development, 1990), p.82
6. Chetna Galla, 'Economic Policy and Panchayat Raj Institutions', (Unpublished report), p.6
7. ibid.
8. Shiviah and Srivastava, ibid, p.46
9. Galla, *Economic Policy*, p.9
10. V. Ramachandran, *Threats to Panchayati Raj Health for the Millions*, (New Delhi: VHAI), p 8
11. Shah and Gandhi, op. cit., p.23
12. 'Partners in Grassroots Democracy', New Delhi: Centre for Women's Development Studies, (1989), p.13
13. D'Lima, op.cit
14. CWDS and F. Ebert Foundation, *Regional Round-Table on Women's Participation in Policy and Decision-Making Process*, Bihar: CWDS and New Delhi: Friedrich Ebert Foundation, (10-11 October 1991), p.5
15. Shah and Gandhi, op.cit., p.19
16. P. Manikyamba, 'Women Presiding Officers at the Tertiary Political Levels: Patterns of Induction and Challenges in Performance', *Journal of Rural Development*, vol. 9 (6) (1990), p.983
17. Kishwar, 'Nature of Women's Mobilisation'
18. Carolyn Moser, 'Gender Planning in the Third World: Meeting Practical and Strategic Needs', *World Development*, vol. 17, no. 11, (1989)

19. Shah and Gandhi, op. cit., p 8
20. L.C. Jain, Women Enter Panchayats, (1992), p.14
21. ibid., p.14
22. D'Lima, op.cit., p.4
23. Kavita, Shobha, Shobita, Kanchan and Sharada, 'Rural Women Speak', *Seminar* 342, 'Economic Policy', (Feb 1988) , p.44
24. Galla, *Economic Policy*
25. Subhash Mendhapurkar, 'Panchayati Raj Bodies and SUTRA's Interventions: Approaches and Strategies', Solan, Himachal Pradesh: Social Uplift Through Rural Action, (1994), p.14
26. Chetna Galla, 'The Empowerment of Women—The Shetkari Sanghatana Experience in Maharashtra', (Unpublished manuscript)
27. ibid.
28. Ramya Subrahmanian, 'Gender, Power and Political Agency: An Agenda for NGOs', Mumbai: Initiatives for Women in Development, (Oct 1993), p.1
29. ibid., p.7
30. Maxine Molyneux, 'Women in Popular Movements: India and Thailand During the Decade of Women', Gail Omvedt ed., United Nations Research Unit for Social Development, (1986)
31. Subrahmanian, 'Gender, Power and Political Agency', p.5

BIBLIOGRAPHY

ALL-WOMEN PANCHAYATS

Editorial. 'All-Women Panchayats', *Indian Express* (30 November 1992)

Gadkari, Subha. 'The Rule of the Second Sex', *Indian Express* (6 Dec 1992)

———. 'All Women in this Panchayat', *Indian Express* (23 Nov 1992)

Galla, Chetna. 'Trying to Give Women Their Due—The Story of Vitner', *Manushi*, 59 (1990)

———. 'The Ladies' Panel', *Manushi*, 42–43 (1987)

———. 'The Empowerment of Women: The Shetkari Sanghatana Experience in Maharashtra', Unpublished (1995)

Kane, Raju. 'Ralegan Siddhi—Green Revolution in a Capsule', *The Independent* (2 May 1990)

News report. 'Panchayat Women Fight Against Odds', *Times of India* (8 July 1990)

News report. 'All-women Panchayat in Ahmednagar District', *Times of India* (10 Dec 1989)

Pangare, Ganesh and Vasudha Pangare. 'From Poverty to Plenty—The Story of Ralegan Siddhi', in *Studies in Ecology and Sustainable Development*, New Delhi: INTACH (1992)

Pereira, Rehina. 'All-women Panchayat Makes History', *Sunday Times of India* (29 Nov 1992)

Singh, Manjeet. 'We Want to Outdo the Males', *The Sunday Observer* (12 Feb 1989)

PANCHAYATI RAJ

Editorial. 'A Voice for the Silent Majority in India', *Down to Earth* (15 July 1989) : 3–4

Galla, Chetna. *Economic Policy and Panchayat Raj Institutions*, Unpublished

Government of India. *Gramin Vikas Newsletter*. Special issue on Panchayati Raj, Ministry of Rural Development, (Jan 1993)

———. *Panchayati Raj Institutions in India* Ministry of Rural Development, (Nov 1991)

———. *Yojana*. Special issue on Panchayati Raj, Ministry of Rural Development. 33,1 & 2 (26 Jan 1989)

Gupta, Tilak D. 'Partyless Polls to Powerless Panchayats', *Economic and Political Weekly* (31 July 1993), 1567–70

Hirway, Indira. 'Panchayati Raj at Crossroads', *Economic and Political Weekly* (22 July 1989), 1663–67

Inamdar, N. R. 'The Changed Face of Village Administration', *Yojana* (16–31 December 1988), 9–12

Institute of Social Sciences. *The Panchayats*. Report of a Panel Discussion Held in New Delhi on 25 September 1991, New Delhi, (1991)

Institute of Social Sciences. 'Panchayati Raj Update', *Monthly Newsletter*, (April–Dec 1994)

Journal of Rural Development. Special issue on Panchayati Raj, Hyderabad: National Institute of Rural Development (NIRD) 10 ,5 (Sept. 1991)

Kothari, Rajni. 'Decentralisation—A Historic Necessity', in *State against Democracy: In Search of Human Governance*', New Delhi: Ajanta Publications, (1989)

Krishnaswamy, K. S. 'For Panchayats the Dawn is Not Yet', *Economic and Political Weekly* (9 Oct 1993), 2183–86

Manor, James. 'Panchayati Raj and Early Warnings of Disasters', *Economic and Political Weekly* (22 May 1993), 1019–20

Mendhapurkar, Subhash. *Panchayati Raj Bodies and SUTRA's Interventions: Approaches and Strategies*, Solan (Himachal Pradesh) : Social Uplift Through Rural Action, (1994)

Nath, V. 'Panchayati Raj: The Promise and The Prospects', *IASSI Quarterly* 8 ,2 (Sept 1989), 134–40

Pal, Mahi. 'A Critical Review of the Maharashtra Panchayats Act 1994', New Delhi: Voluntary Action Network of India (VANI), 1994

Samanta, R. K. 'The Political Economy of Panchayats in West Bengal' *Social Change*, 20, 2 (May 1990)

'Panchayati Raj', *Journal of Rural Development* 7, 6 (Nov 1988), 689–700

Shahane, V. P. 'Village Panchayats in Maharashtra', *Lokrajya*, Independence Day Number (1988)

Shivaramu, K. and M. B. Channegowda. 'Attitude of Members of Mandal Panchayats Towards Mandal Panchayats', *Journal of Rural Development* 10, 3 (May 1991), 333–41

Shiviah, M. *Panchayati Raj: A Policy Perspective*, Hyderabad: National Institute of Rural Development (NIRD), 1986

Shiviah, M. and K. B. Srivastava. *Factors Affecting Development of the Panchayati Raj System*, Hyderabad: National Institute of Rural Development (NIRD), 1990

Singh, S. K. 'Development and Gram Panchayat: A Case Study of Rajsamadhiyala Gram Panchayat', *Journal of Rural Development* 12, 1 (May 1993), 541–45

Singh, Surat. 'Constitutional Safeguards to Enhance the Status of Panchayati Raj Institutions', *Journal of Rural Development* 12, 1 (Jan 1993), 77–88

Singh, Surat and C. A. Rahim. 'Evolving Panchayati Raj Leadership', *Journal of Rural Development* 8, 4 (July 1989), 415–29

Society for Participatory Research in Asia (PRIA). 'In Pursuit of Local Self-Governance: Training Modules for Panchayati Raj', New Delhi : PRIA (April 1994)

LEGAL ASPECTS

The Bombay Village Panchayats Act, (1958)
The Maharashtra Zilla Parishads and Panchayat Samitis Act, (1961)

WOMEN AND PANCHAYATI RAJ

Arora, Diva. 'Power to the Woman', *The Statesman* (17 April 1993)

Athale, Gouri Agtey. 'Women in the Driver's Seat', *Indian Express* (13 October 1993)

Bose, Noyona. 'Creating Political Viragos?', *The Statesman* (17 April 1993)

D. N. 'Reservations for Women in Panchayats', *Economic and Political Weekly* (10 June 1989)

D'Lima, Hazel. 'The Participation of Women in Local Self-Government', Mumbai: Nirmala Niketan College of Social Work, (1984)

Dam, Marcus. 'The Burden of Being Women Panchayat Members', *The Statesman* (25 Oct 1993)

Deshmukh, Vinita. 'Ostracised, Beaten, Because She's a Woman Sarpanch', *Indian Express* (10 March 1994)

Forum for Women in Panchayati Raj. Meeting Report, 11 May 1993, New Delhi : Friedrich Ebert Stiftung, (1993)

Galla, Chetna. Women in Panchayats. *Manushi* 65, 3-6

Gawankar, Rohini. 'Female Representation in Panchayat Raj Institutions in the State of Maharashtra', *New Quest* (May–June 1985)

Gopalan, Sarala. 'Women in Panchayati Raj', *Uma Prachar*, New Delhi and Bangalore: Institute of Social Studies Trust, (Jan–Dec 1994)

Lele, Medha Kotwal and Simrita Gopal Singh. 'Women in Local Self-Government in Maharashtra: Implications for Empowerment of Women', Pune: Aalochana, (1993)

Manikyamba, P. 'Women Presiding Officers at the Tertiary Political Levels: Patterns of Induction and Challenges in Performance', *Journal of Rural Development* 9 ,6 (1990), 983–94

Mathew, George. 'Beginning of a Silent Revolution', *The Hindu* (18 Dec 1993)

———. 'A Vote for Women in Orissa', *Indian Express* (20 July 1992)

Mitra, Amit. 'Will Women in Panchayats Transform Bengal?', *Down to Earth* (15 July 1993)

Mukhopadhyay, Ashim. 'Seventy- Third Amendment, Panchayati Raj and Women', *Frontier* (22 Jan 1994)

Nagaraja, Bhargavi. 'Karnataka Halts Mahila Empowerment', *Indian Express* (31 Jan 1992)

News report. 'Male Domination in Karnataka Mandal Panchayats', *Financial Express* (9 Feb 1991)

News report. 'Seats Reserved for Women in Bengal', *The Telegraph* (26 June 1992)

Omvedt, Gail. 'Women, Zilla Parishads and Panchayati Raj—Chandwad to Vitner', *Economic and Political Weekly* (4 August 1990), 1687-90

———. 'Peasants and Women—Challenge of Chandwad', *Economic and Political Weekly* (29 November 1986), 2085–86

Prasad, Leela Devi. *Reservation for Women Participants in Local and State-Level Bodies of Political Parties in Karnataka*, New Delhi: Centre for Social Research, (1991)

Rai, Usha. 'Political Empowerment in Top Gear', *Indian Express* (3 March 1993)

Sawhney, Inder. 'MP Shows Way in Empowering Women', *Times of India* (8 March 1995)

SEARCH. 'Training Support to Women in Panchayati Raj Institutions', *Search News*, 9, 1 (Jan-March 1994)

———. 'Panchayati Raj and Women', *Search News*, 8, 1 and 2 (Jan-Jun 1993)

Shashikala, S. 'Caste and Age Factors Count', *Deccan Herald* (1 June 1991)

———. 'Women's Role in ZP Beset with Hurdles', *Deccan Herald* (21 Jan 1991)

Society for Promotion of Area Resource Centres (SPARC). 'Planning for Panchayati Raj: A Workshop Report', Mumbai, (1994)

Tata Institute of Socia Sciences (TISS). 'Report of the Workshop on Role of Women in Panchayati Raj, 30–31 March 1990', Mumbai: TISS, 1990

WOMEN AND POLITICS

Anklesaria, Shahnaz. 'Women as Agents of Social Change', *The Statesman* (14 February 1990)

Balasubrahmanyam, Vimal. 'Women Don't Need Quota', *Mainstream* (18 May 1991)

Centre for Women's Development Studies (CWDS). Report : Regional Round-Table on Womens Participation in Policy and Decision-Making Process, 10-11 October 1991, New Delhi : CWDS and Friedrich Ebert Foundation.

Chatterji, Shoma. 'The Woman Vote—Does It Really Count?' *Free Press Journal* (26 May 1991)

Freindrich Ebert Stifung (FES). *Women in Politics: Forms and Processes*. New Delhi : FES, (1992)

Gandhi, Nandita and Nandita Shah, . *The Quota Question* (a monograph), Mumbai : Akshara, (1991)

Gorhe, Neelam. *Issues About Women And Politics*, Pune: Stree Aadhar Kendra, (1991)

Joshi, Meera. 'Women Want Quota in Legislatures', *Times of India* (17 May 1992)

Khan, Sakina Yusuf. 'Sorry, It's a Stag Party', *Times of India* (19 May 1991)

Kishwar, Madhu. 'Sidelined', *Illustrated Weekly of India* (4 February 1990)

Manor, James. 'Positive Trends in Indian Politics', *Sunday Times of India* (19 March 1995)

Mazumdar, Vina. 'Reservations for Women', *Economic and Political Weekly* (16 December 1989), 2795–96

Menon, Meena. 'Consciousness Rising in Ratnagiri', *Times of India* (1 May 1991)

Nelson, Barbara and Najma Chowdhury. *Women and Politics Worldwide* New Haven: Yale University Press, (1994)

Newspaper clippings. 'Women and Electoral Politics 1990-1994', Aalochana, Pune, 1995.

News report. 'Women's Accession to Power Very Slow: ILO', *Times of India* (9 March 1993)

News report. 'Women in Politics Bereft of Powers', *Times of India* (17 February 1993)

News report. 'Women Have Little Say in Shaping Policy - UN', *Times of India* (21 June 1991)

News report. Indian Women's Involvement in Elections Disappoints', *The Independent* (24 October 1989)

Patel, Vibhuti. Getting a Foothold in Politics. In *Readings on Women Studies* Series, no. 5, Mumbai: Research Centre for Women's Studies, SNDT University

———. 'Reaching for Half the Sky', *The Hindu* (30 February 1990)

Philipose, Pamela. 'Do Women Constitute a Vote Bank?' *The Business and Political Observer* (12 April 1991)

Radhika, K. 'An Opportunity for Genuine Empowerment', *The Sunday Observer* (1 Aug 1993)

Ramaswamy, Sushila. 'Women Marginalised', *Indian Express* (26 Jan 1994)

Research Centre for Women's Studies, SNDT University. 'India—Women and Politics', *Women's International Network News* 18-1 (Winter 1992)

——— *Women in Decision-Making*, Mumbai: SNDT University, (1991)

Seoul Statement: Empowering Women in Politics, (1992)

Sharma, Kalpana. 'The Men Decide for Them' *The Hindu* (19 May 1991)

———. 'The Other Half', *Times of India* (10 June 1989)

———. 'Women at the Hustings', *Indian Express* (23 October 1988)

Subrahmanian, Ramya. 'Gender, Power and Political Agency: An Agenda for NGOs', Initiatives for Women in Development, Mumbai, (October 1993)

WOMEN

Bhave, Sumitra. *Pan on Fire*, New Delhi: Indian Social Institute, (1988)

Desai, Neera. 'Caste, Class and Gender', Mumbai: SNDT Women's University, Dept of Sociology